OWNERLESS EARTH

OWNERLESS EARTH

EARTH

New & Selected Poems

Michael Hamburger

E. P. Dutton & Co., Inc. | New York | 1973

1950, 1952, 1958, 1963, 1969, 1973
Copyright © by Michael Hamburger
All rights reserved. Printed in England
First Edition

Published simultaneously in Canada
by Clarke, Irwin & Company Limited, Toronto and Vancouver

Library of Congress Catalog Number: 72-95548
SBN 0-525-17435-4

The author wishes to thank the editors of the following publications, in which
his poems have appeared: *Agenda, Aquarius, Chelsea* (USA), *Decal, The Guardian,
Poetry Book Society Supplement, Poetry Review, Stand, Sumac* (USA), *Tagus, Vortex,*
and *Wave*, among others. Special acknowledgement is due to *Poetry* for permission
to reprint two sections of the 'Travelling' sequence which first appeared there

The following poems Copyright © Michael Hamburger 1969 are from *Travelling,*
by permission of Fulcrum Press. *Travelling* is in print and published by Fulcrum Press
'In Philistia' 'For no one' 'The Other Day' 'Memory' 'Theogony' 'The Blight'
'S-Bahn' 'Homo Sum' 'New Goddess' 'Orpheus Street' 'Loach' 'Oxford' 'Friends'
'At Fifty-five' 'Dowland' 'For a Family Album' 'Grey Heat' 'The House Martins'
'The Jackdaws' and 'Travelling I'

CONTENTS

Author's Note

I USED TO wonder why some poets have preferred to have selections from their work made by other people. Now I know. The very meagre representation here of poems from my first two collections has to do with one difficulty I came up against – that of relating myself to work done by a writer altogether different from the one I now feel myself to be. Since that writer used my name I couldn't be quite fair to him, let alone 'objective' in my judgement of what he wrote. I may well have rejected poems by him that are better made, more finished, than some of the later pieces I have included; but, if so, those more finished pieces don't interest me, and I have no use for them now.

Another difficulty I came up against is that a strictly chronological order, an order based on successive collections, didn't strike me as the best one, except in the case of *The Dual Site*. I have never been able to plan or predict what sort of poems I might be writing at any time in the near or not so near future, what themes and forms I had done with, which would recur. When I published the poem *Travelling* in the collection of that name I had no idea that a second and third part would follow some two years after the first. The only sensible thing to do was to let the selection find its own order, even if this meant some untidy overlapping from book to book. New or uncollected poems, therefore, occur in several sections, together with collected ones to which they are related.

Very few textual alterations have been made for this selection, though some earlier revisions and excisions have been taken over.

Michael Hamburger

I
Projections
1941-1951

PADDINGTON CANAL

A mocking mirror, the black water turns
Tall houses upside down, makes learned men
Walk on their heads in squares of burning light;
Lovers like folded bats hang in a kiss,
Swaying as if a breeze could sever them.
The barges, giant sea-birds fast asleep,
Lie on the surface, moored and motionless;
Then, drowning gently, are drawn down to join
The sunken lovers and the acrobats.
Out of the grim dimensions of a street
Slowly I see another landscape grow
Downwards into a lost reality;
A magic mirror, the black water tells
Of a reversed Atlantis wisely built
To catch and to transform
The wasted substance of our daily acts,
Accommodate our mad and lovely doubles
In a more graceful city timelessly.

Like snooker balls thrown on the table's faded green,
Rare ivory and weighted with his best ambitions,
At first his words are launched: not certain what they mean,
He loves to see them roll, rebound, assume positions
Which – since not he – some higher power has assigned.
But now the game begins: dead players, living critics
Are watching him – and suddenly one eye goes blind,
The hand that holds the cue shakes like a paralytic's,
Till every thudding, every clinking sound portends
New failure, new defeat. Amazed, he finds that still
It is not he who guides his missiles to their ends
But an unkind geometry that mocks his will.

If he persists, for years he'll practise patiently,
Lock all the doors, learn all the tricks, keep noises out,
Though he may pick a ghost or two for company
Or pierce the rooms inhuman silence with a shout.
More often silence wins; then soon the green felt seems
An evil playground, lawless, lost to time, forsaken,
And he a fool caught in the water weeds of dreams
Whom only death or frantic effort can awaken.

At last, a master player, he can face applause,
Looks for a fit opponent, former friends, emerges;
But no one knows him now. He questions his own cause,
And has forgotten why he yielded to those urges,
Took up a wooden cue to strike a coloured ball.
Wise now, he goes on playing; both his house and heart
Unguarded solitudes, hospitable to all
Who can endure the cold intensity of art.

THE DEATH OF AN OLD MAN

Muttering at the crowd, indifferent
Faces which could not understand that he,
An island full of wilting flowers pent
In by the foolish, the forgetting sea,
Was rare and beautiful, quite suddenly
He plunged into the traffic, his neck bent
Low like a fighting bull's who seems intent
On the quick blade but, bleeding, cannot see.

Then he awoke, his body broken, knew
What had happened. In the dusk his mind
Began its last descent, let pain review
The landscape he could neither leave behind
Nor take away; for who will now unwind
His memory, relive past love, renew
The music and the silences that grew
Within him for a life-time, intertwined?

HÖLDERLIN

Tübingen, December 1842

Diotima is dead, and silent
The island's singing bird.
The temple I raised from ruin
Fallen again.

Where is the flame I stoked from ashes
Of the mind? Where are the heroes
And my pulsing song?
Nothing stirs on the lakes of time.
Give back my agony,
O stir the forest's sap,
Sweep my slow blood.

And yet, no caged old panther I,
Pacing my madness. These muttered words
Are gates, not bars, where only I can pass.
This is my wisdom, where no flowers grow,
No weeds, this is my peace.

I am calm now, with the world
Locked out, bowed to the door;
My meadow end is pensioned by the gods.
They did not hear,
O crippled Fate, the grimy idol's
Golden teeth led them away.

I have no tears to mourn forsaken gods
Or my lost voice.
This is my wisdom where no laughter sounds,
No sighs, this is my peace.

Glory is gone, and the swimming clouds;
My dumb hand grips the frozen sky,
A black bare tree in the winter dusk.

'THE TEMPEST'

An Alternative

I, Prospero, stand on this island's shore,
And from a distance vaguer and more dubious
Than a dream I hear voices as of lovers
Whispering in the night and courtiers jesting.

I recall a tempest that created peace;
But the power that brought forth storms and stillness
Is quite decayed, so they have left me here,
An old man with a bent back, who has outlived
His death.
      Yes, once they called me prince,
(Though then my pride lay elsewhere) until I fled
And made this isle my kingdom, ruling by magic.

I recall a tempest raised for the sake
Of a mortal throne, a night and a day
Of mortal music . . . and then this stillness.

Now I bear logs for Caliban whose lust
Has peopled the isle with monsters, begotten
On my daughter; sweet Miranda's grown a hag
With hatching of his slimy progeny.

Perhaps it was a dream (the human voices
And my hoping to follow them) – and a mere dream
Has made me weary – but my master calls, –
I'm coming Caliban. – One night, one day
Lost me my dukedom and my soul's wide realm,
Ariel deserted me and they left me here.

T. S. ELIOT

A Tribute

Almost it was too late, near closing-time
For Europe when he came to gather up
Whatever petals wind and broom had spared
In the last garden; there it was he heard
The laughter of belated children leap
Before the outraged keeper sent them home.

Then it was night; a sprawling town stretched out
Sick limbs where temporary lovers walked,
While in the distance dying trumpeters
Blared insult and self-pity at the stars.
He studied patience; and when next he looked.
Some kind of dawn quivered on dirty slate.

JUDAS ISCARIOT

No part was harder than his and none more cruel:
To be God's chosen villain in the absolute play,
Cast out by friends and enemies, cast out of self,
Hated by all for ever, hating himself;
And that the sinous prophecy might be fulfilled,
Wriggle, a viper, down the appointed path,
Dust on his tongue,
Till he was dry and twisted as the final rope.

Pilate could speak of duty, Peter of human fear
Keener than love; but Judas could not speak,
For he had ripped out fear with the roots of love
And his inhuman duty was unspeakable.
Dust in his heart,
The inmost source of language clogged with dust,
He dreamed of sleep,
How in the end one drowsy snake would meet another,
Coiled in a dumb, yet passionate embrace.

That was the second kiss;
The first – how long ago it seemed – had killed him.
Might not the second give him life again?
Myopic men would hate him – so the play demanded –
But would the Master who gazed with different eyes?
A maze, a mystery was justice; only this he knew:
In God's own forge he had been melted down,
By God's own hammer beaten into murderous shape,
Betrayed into betraying.
After the deed, might not the instrument rest?

Or could it be that when the curtain fell on the last scene,
When, silent, the spectators stumbled home,
Still the actors were not dismissed, but in the dark
Must re-enact their parts?
If it was true that shroud and sepulchre could not contain
The Master's fiery spirit,
Then he for ever too, as Christ was Christ,
For ever must be Judas
And in a hell of cold self-hatred bite his tail.

Sleep, then, would be no refuge: never would he shed
His dark imprisoning skin, the dust of that long day,
Nor ever in the sweet still water bathe.

A BRIEF BIOGRAPHY

This poor amphibian on the dry land of prose
Watched others labour; now hoped to emulate
The troubled ant who, gathering details, goes
Patiently about his business, to create;
Now sickened by the sight, he envied fish –
Whose yielding element, it seemed, fulfilled
Their faintest, mute unformulated wish
Lest impulse should grow weak by being willed –
For foolishly, deliciously intent
On self-expression, all day long they played
In the clear liquid of abandonment,
Poetic palaces of light and shade . . .
Then with the ducks became identified,
Domestic, democratic, sociable,
Not over-clean, but innocent of pride,
Products of humble homesteads and the Fall . . .
Till he saw swans – a pair of them – and knew:
Art is aristocratic. Lend me pure white
To glide on time's calm waters or in the blue
Expanse of summer answer the infinite!

Oh, he was none of these; could scarcely swim,
Not walk at all, nor fly, nor work, nor play.
What most he loved most cruelly wounded him
By being loveliest when he turned away.
He could sit still for hours, catch a few flies –
A modest minimum – on his floating log,
But soon would languish for the great surprise,
Proof that he was not what he was, a frog.

Ants climbed and stumbled, fell and climbed once more,
The leisured fishes glittered in glassy streams,
Ducks paddled, dived or waddled on the shore,
The swans, two distant lovers, guarded their dreams.
He gazed and hoped and envied, rarely tried,
Yet, always changing, giddily revolved,
Restless till in the unremembering tide
His tortured multiplicity dissolved.

LINES ON BRUEGHEL'S ICARUS

The ploughman ploughs, the fisherman dreams of fish;
Aloft, the sailor through a world of ropes
Guides tangled meditations, feverish
With memories of girls forsaken, hopes
Of brief reunions, new discoveries,
Past rum consumed, rum promised, rum potential.
Sheep crop the grass, lift up their heads and gaze
Into a sheepish present: the essential,
Illimitable juiciness of things,
Greens, yellows, browns are what they see.
Churlish and slow, the shepherd, hearing wings –
Perhaps an eagle's – gapes uncertainly;

Too late. The worst had happened: lost to man,
The angel, Icarus, for ever failed,
Fallen with melted wings when, near the sun
He scorned the ordering planet, which prevailed
And jeering, now slinks off, to rise once more.
But he – his damaged purpose drags him down –
Too far from his half-brothers on the shore,
Hardly conceivable, is left to drown.

II
The Dual Site
1952-1957

PALINODE

A daily vision broke my rage:
The beauty of a cold white page,
Bare island in a polar sea
Whose terrible virginity
A hymen of deep ice defends.
Here the familiar voyage ends;
But, though becalmed, at last I know
The heat that radiates from snow.
    Flies on the window-pane,
    My words have buzzed in vain.

Or southern landscapes: child and nun
Turned into objects by the sun;
All emptied by a light so strong
That on the hill the ploughman's song
Was no less natural than the breeze
That bore it through the olive-trees.
Harsh as blue grapes, his voice conveyed
Dark due to sunshine, not to shade.
    An animal's ecstasy or pain,
    Ambiguous, echoed through the plain.

And there a bullfight purged the heart
Of comforts fiction adds to art,
Applying Aristotle's law,
Pity and terror, in the raw:
This hero's flesh confirmed the plot.
No, never Jove, nor Juggernaut
Smiled on the trembling jade that bore
Pain's padded priest, the picador.
    Where gushing blood is plain
    Will sand absorb the stain?

Recant, recant the tenderness
That flows too easily. Confess:
Well shod against the jagged stalk
We tender-footed poets walk
On horrors multiple as grass,

A luscious carpet – pause, but pass;
And like the matador's, our skill
Is wasted if we cannot kill.
       Loud in the weather-vane
       Unfeeling winds complain.

Kill every creature, beast and bird,
Flower and ourselves, to feed the Word,
Our last Chimaera never found
Till we have covered desert ground
With serpents, goats, and lions killed
For the one site on which to build
An egocentric heap of stones
Inscribed: Bellerophon – his bones.
       Yet not for so much gain:
       Vanished summits we attain.

To climb and voyage in the heat
Prepared me for a worse defeat:
This last and loveliest anchorage
Where a cold summer broke my rage.
Explorers dying here, on seas
Rigid with Time's own cruelties,
Gasped out another vision too:
A town . . . white marble . . . veined with blue.
       Lost is the song in the plain;
       Raked in the blood-red stain;
       Silent the weather-vane.

THE SACRIFICE

'We are not deathless but you make us so,
Being the dreadful Emperor for whose sake
We are about to die and dying seek
None but a posthumous honour, your applause,
No boon but his you've granted us, a cause:
Your dubious distance from the men we know.'

Distant indeed, that Emperor is gone,
And long before his fall had ceased to note
Whose was the point and whose the punctured throat,
Bored past endurance with their martyrdom.
The plebs alone gave every face a name,
Counting the wounds he would not look upon.

Now some went wild because afraid to doubt,
So wild, they could not wait until the day,
But mauled their guards and died without delay.
Others, unfit for arms, were loosed in packs
To pitch their bulk at undefended backs
Though whores and hangmen hissed the knockabout.

The best betrayed suspicion in a twist
Lent to the formal greeting, showed the skill
Of nonchalant courage, but grew loath to kill.
The cause held good: present or absent, he –
More than himself – must bless their agony;
And, bad at murder, here they'd not be missed.

The Emperor's usurper, too, is dead.
But even now, they say, from time to time
A good man wins and, punished for that crime
In contravention of the ancient laws,
Hears ghostly words grow faint, the god's applause,
Dying in doubt, yet strangely comforted.

PHILOCTETES

The sky grows dumb, the seasons of my pain
Are not the mainland seasons.
Contracted in this wound my thought grows blind
And I blaspheme
Because the island of my wound is loud.
Now that I doubt this bow's divinity
I am the beasts I feed in, less than the birds
That only visit here, though here they fall
Pierced by my hated arrows.

Once I could picture archipelagos,
Prayed to the binding sea
To grant me news of those I left behind,
News of my father and of Heracles,
The living and the dead.
The sea grows dumb and I grow separate,
Confined to Lemnos where the tide is pain,
A festering foot the seasons –
Now that I doubt this wound's divinity.

Once I could search the clouds for images,
Could strain my eyes for some redeeming voice
Vouchsafed by Heracles –
The sun's blind eye moved in a labyrinth
And sparks of no great fire the stars went out.
No message, but the stillness of despair,
Dumb rocks, the deafened sea,
And every cry my separate agony,
Cacophonous echo in my stinking lair.

Wrong after wrong, the prowling cats of the sea:
Tricked by a mortal, here ends prophecy:
If by Odysseus' cunning Troy is taken
In godless peace Hellas will waste away –
Now numb, now sore – their fate
To live on Lemnos, long for Thessaly
Till in the glutinous air
No bird can break their seasons and no prayer
Travel towards the mainland of their pain.

NARCISSUS

Not he was beautiful, nor yet the other
Whose lustre guarded darkness on the pool –
Too much himself, too near to him for love –
But somewhere in between
Its image-haunted surface and the bed
A face grew beautiful and approved his love.

At first she would not come,
As if afraid of his or the other's face –
The other's it must be, for him she loved –
Then, as he waited, suddenly was there,
Such longing in her eyes as his for her
But inaccessible always,
Her lips beyond his reach, even her outstretched arms,
Though once he felt the touch of her fingertips,
Unbearable in that stillness, and could not stay.

But what he fled from questioned why he fled:
Where, when she came, was he, his daylight double ?
He whom they said he loved
And gladly would have loved if love allowed
Such easy self-completion
As between stalk and shadow would be natural,
These rushes and their complement on the pool.
No, like the water-lily's leaves he lay
Too near the would-be mirror of himself,
Leaving no space for comfort in self-love,
Full day above, no light but hers below.

That other, then, must blur
And vanish back into himself when she
Gathered and drew him down into the dark
And in the alien element he saw
Her streaming hair, a nymph's, and not the other's.

Likeness there was perhaps; and yet no more
Than if his sister – like him to a stranger
But not to him who used no looking-glass –

Outgrowing all his memories and his grief
By change in death had learnt
To hide behind a lovelier woman's gaze.

Now from that gaze he fled and could not flee,
In heavy half-sleep nightly must repeat
The waiting and the meeting, till the touch
Of icy-finger-tips shivered his flesh awake
Or plunging through her stunned him into sense.

To venture back seemed best; the silence loud
In daylight, and his double there to taunt him
Until he dared to look.
A moorhen shrieked; far off an eagle swooped and struck.
A dragonfly rattled faintly, dipped and for a moment broke
The surface of his frailty, rippling the other's face,
So that he smiled, though still the other stared,
His eyes two troubled pools within the pool.

Now, lingering, almost tenderly for once,
Narcissus took his leave, dismissed his double,
Entered those pools and sinking, sinking left
All thought of day behind him,
Could hear no sound, forgot to feel the sun,
Grew cool as water, one with water, flowed,
Slowed down when from a single pool his eyes
Diverged once more in halflight, then moved on
Towards the darkness where two points of light
Fused with himself would quench him and be quenched . . .

Then he remembered: motionless on the bank
He'd left his body, motionless the other
Watched him and aped him there;
He turned about to end that mockery,
Rose up while she, receding, grew distinct;
Seeing her whole, he loosened, she rose up
To meet his fall half-way.
Clasped in her arms, entangled in her hair,
Eyes, lips and body fast, Narcissus drowned.

* * *

Strange, but the only witness, a young girl,
Crept from her hiding-place on the opposite bank
To swear she'd seen Narcissus bend his head
Over his own reflected self and kiss
None but the pool's cold mouth,
Rise on his arms, slide forward and slide down,
So slow, so quiet and so natural,
She had not stirred until the surface closed,
The last small ripple vanished.

Why had she hidden there? She would not tell,
But said again: as natural, as complete
As water-irises and their complement on the pool
Only more beautiful in that symmetry
Because Narcissus still, and more than flower;
And yet not quite Narcissus:
For poised above his image on the water,
Too much himself, he'd left no space for love,
Remote from her as heron, crane, or swan,
Rooted in his own stillness like a flower.

THE DUAL SITE

To my twin who lives in a cruel country
   I wrote a letter at last;
For my bones creaked out in our long silence
   That seven years had passed,

Seven whole years since he and I
   By word or token exchanged
The message I dare not do without:
   That still we are not estranged,

Though I watch figures in a city office
   And he the waves of the sea,
Keeping no count since he hardly cares
   What happens to him or to me;

Since to names and numbers he closed his head
   When, children still, we were parted,
Chose birth and death for his calendar,
   But leaves the dates uncharted,

Being one who forgets what I remember,
   Who knows what I do not,
Who has learnt the ways of otter and raven
   While I've grown polyglot.

Lately I found a cactus in flower
   And feared for his apple-trees,
Dozed in the club and saw his cattle
   Drag with a foul disease,

And my bones grown stiff with leaning and lying
   Cried out that I'll labour in vain
Till I help my twin to rebuild his hovel
   That's open to wind and rain.

So I sent him a note, expecting no answer,
   And a cheque he'd never cash,
For I knew he was one who'd smile if he heard
   His own roof come down with a crash,

But above the porpoise-leaping bay
  Where ploughshare fin and tail
Cut furrows the foam-flecked sea fills up
  He'd stand in the swishing gale,

Calm as the jackdaws that nest in crannies
  And no more prone to doubt,
With gull and cormorant perched on the rocks
  Would wait the weather out.

Yet he wrote by return: 'Have no fear for your dwelling
  Though dry-rot gnaws at the floors;
Only lighten their load of marble and metal,
  Keep clear the corridors,

Move out the clocks that clutter your study,
  And the years will leave you alone:
Every frame I know of lasts long enough,
  Though but cardboard, wood or bone.

And spare me your nightmares, brother, I beg you,
  They make my daemons laugh,
They scare the spirits that rarely will visit
  A man with no wand or staff,

With no symbol, no book and no formula,
  No lore to aid him at all,
Who wherever he walks must find the image
  That holds his mentors in thrall.

But your waking cares put down on paper
  For me to give to the wind,
That the seed may fall and the dry leaf crumble,
  Not a wisp be left behind

Of the tangle that hides the dual site
  Where even you and I
Still may meet again and together build
  One house before we die.'

A CHILD ACCEPTS

'Later', his mother said; and still those little hands
Clawed air to clutch the object of their need,
Abandoned as birds to winds or fishes to tide,
Pure time that is timeless, time untenanted.

'Later', she said; and the word was cold with death,
Opposing space to his time, intersecting his will.
He summoned the cry of a wounded animal,
Mindless Adam whose world lies crushed by the Fall,

But suddenly mended his face and far from tears
Grew radiant, relaxed, letting his hands drop down.
'Later', he sang, and was human, fallen again,
Received into mind, his dubious, his true demesne.

'Later', he played with the word, and later will envy
The freedom of birds and fishes for ever lost,
When, migrant in mind whom wind and water resist,
Here he must winter in body, bound to the coast;

Or, not all his 'laters' past, perhaps he'll know
That the last releases: reversed, his needs will throng
Homeward to nest in his head and breed among
Those hidden rocks that wrecked him into song.

MAN IN A GARDEN

Creation's monster, metaphysical man
Across the garden moves his soft machine,
Propelled by timeless fuel, caught in time,
Changing, unchanging, mobile, half at home . . .
His legs in Croydon, head for Eden bound,
Between two stars he tills the promised land.

A budding snowdrop beckons to his eyes:
'As flower in soil, so mind in body grows,
Wept by the primal dark' . . . He tastes the weather,
Sweet on the tongue, loosening his lips to gather
Breezes like manna; but his lungs expel
Polluted vapour, warm and personal.
He listens: blackbirds fluting . . . pigeons talking;
But in his entrails hears a time-bomb ticking,
Planted at birth, set for the mocking hour.
Screaming, a sea-mew hurtles through the air:
'Birdsong is praise because a bird can die;
We do not leave but take the world away,
The world that's in us, falling when we fall:
Almost we dare not live our lives at all.'

And still he digs, digs in his grievance there,
Long after dusk; digs till his mind is bare
Yet in its bareness holds one metaphor:
'Stars in the dark and out of soil a flower.'

TRAVELLERS

For Edwin Muir on his 70th Birthday

Some travel to lose their way; the glib and loud,
Boasting their bag, experience, in miles and days.
From sea to sea they roar, from coast to coast,
From lover to lover.
All that they praise is their own bloodstream flowing,
All that they rage at the benzedrine of the blood,
Faster than mind, their zest and their undoing.
Bored by the flora, they do not learn,
But alienate, lay waste what they discover,
Trapped in the machinations of their quest;
Can conquer but not colonize; roam but not explore.
Now climb a high peak, now dive deep for corals,
Now hunt a beast no living man has faced—
In the wrong season, with the wrong gun.
Brought close by chance to the one answering shore,
Hot hungry eyes they fix on it unseeing
While the ship moves on;
Remember no home and never return.

Another in the cabin's lamplight quietly
Construes the country where he has not been,
Waits for the envisaged bay to realize,
Easily lands and thinks his way
To a familiar city, pre-possessed.
All, all he recognizes; every tree's position,
The shapes of bridges, colour of local stone,
Moods of the sky and mode of each bird's flying;
From faces, gestures, words overheard retraces
The legend of his trials, his acquittals:,
Reads how he was not wise nor brave
Till seven times shipwrecked, seven times saved,
And could not act and could not see
Till seven times blinded, seven times healed,
Battered into identity.

RIVER SONG

Not proud to row but glad to glide
Leave the certainties of earth,
Leave the doubts of earth and ride
The dimpled surface of this tide,
Element of Love's own birth.

Cygnets, ducklings do not know
What purpose launches them on glass,
How wide and long the currents flow
In the muddy bed below,
But reflected, unreflecting, pass.

Haphazard as convolvulus
Wind your thoughts, apply your hand,
Like these fluttering flowers trace
Mad patterns on the mirror's face,
Lightly glide and lightly land.

BANKRUPT

Living above his means for all those years
He had no choice but in the end must honour
The world that honours every gay pretence;
Feasted rich friends for fear of poverty
And when his creditors called must turn them into debtors
Who'd count it gain to drink at his expense
And lend him more: hard cash and flattery
To keep the party going.
                  Long they'd thought:
'Fear too can fix a firm economy.
Here's one so set in weakness, count on him;
If move he must, will take such care of comfort,
He'll never feel the change – and nor shall we.
True, he looks haggard, but can face no mirror,
Is growing lean, but dare not know his weight.'

It was his conscience dunned him, while they fawned,
Though without cause as yet they sensed betrayal.
From street to street he dodged it, and they followed,
Remarking this chair was new, that picture gone,
The room more crowded and the carpet thinner;
Yet wine and wit flowed freely as before.

At last (removals make us) he could laugh again
Unprompted by their faces and, alone,
Prepared to pay his ransom, vanish from that city.
'But lest in vain I shed sweet vanity,'
Because the cure could breed a worse disease, he prayed,
'Salt the dry crust and keep the sour fruit pure.
To queens once exiled, my dear guests a while,
But reinstated now, I'll send no humble greetings,
Hoping despite myself for crumbs of favour.
Yet when forgetfulness is my discipline –
Which, granted strength enough, I'll not relax –
Still I'll need wealth to keep a sole friend faithful,
Such peace as will permit me to recall:
Moved by whose grace into a dingy house.'

SPRING SONG IN WINTER

Too long, too long
I gathered icicles in spring
To thread them for a melting song;
And in midsummer saw the foliage fall,
Too foolish then to sing
How leaf and petal cling
Though wind would bear them to the root of all.

Now winter's come, and winter proves me wrong:
Dark in my garden the dead
Great naked briars, have spread,
So vastly multiplied
They almost hide
The single shrub to share whose blossoming
Blood on cold thorns my fingers shed.

AFTER CHRISTMAS

Gone is that errant star. The shepherds rise
And, packed in buses, go their separate ways
To bench and counter where their flocks will graze
On winter grass, no bonus of sweet hay.
The myrrh, the frankincense fade from memory:
Another year of waiting for the day.

Still in his palace Herod waits for orders:
Arrests, an edict, more judicial murders,
New taxes, reinforcements for the borders.
Still high priests preach decorum, rebels rage
At Caesar battening on their heritage
And a few prophets mourn a godless age.

The Magi in three chauffeur-driven cars
Begin their homeward journey round the wars,
Each to his capital, the stocks and shares
Whose constellations, flickering into place,
Must guide him through a vaster wilderness
Than did the star absconded out of space.

The golden thread winds back upon the spool.
A bird's dry carcass and an empty bottle
Beside the dustbin, vomit of goodwill,
Pale streets, pale faces and a paler sky;
A paper Bethlehem, a rootless tree
Soon to be stripped, dismembered, put away,

Burnt on the grate . . . and dressed in candlelight
When next the shepherds turn their flocks about,
The three wise kings recall their second state
And from the smaller circle of the year,
Axle and weighted hub, look high and far
To pierce their weekday heaven that hides the star.

DIALOGUE

'Tell us again of love and death,
Opposed, that we may picture both
Who cannot think them separate.
Death a mere empty frame we hate
And only love
At one remove:
So giddied by the turning wheel,
We need a mirror, loss, to see the loved one whole.'

'Never again, since she
First breathing on the mirror hid
The macrocosmic mystery,
To leave us lost; till newly centred, grown
More partial, we should need
No other loss to prove
The wholeness of your love,
Nor any quickening discord but our own.'

EARLY LOVE

i

Hot in cold armour from his moated youth
He ventures out, less ignorant of death
Than of the temporal town's complexities,
Whorl, criss-cross and ellipse. Of love he knows
A peak long wondered at, disdains the slopes
Because a stranger yet to all mishaps
But headlong thought's abysses, hell in dream.
Now far from both the boundaries of his home,
Garden and moss-damp forest, he must brave
Ambiguous ways, the heart's alternative,
Moderate heights to climb with bleeding shins
And where he treads, the clatter of small stones.

ii

Nothing is single there, and nothing pure:
Mind mixed with flesh, as animal with flower,
As flower with rock; and all dissimilar.

Nymph to his satyr, Psyche to his ghost
She lures him to division, at her cost:
(Darkness was daylight when the nightly god,
Nameless, illumined Psyche: dark, he glowed
Until to light his radiance was betrayed.)
No master, in the darkness of their tryst –
Meeting unlit by moon or memory –
He falters, gropes, and falls; she fades away,
Dark as the night, in unreality.

(A nymph, more weed than woman, water weed,
Bends to the current, fashioned to be swayed,
Blossoms above, her floor the river bed.)
No diver yet, he drags her image down
To drown it in that depth; back in the sun –
Too bright – he blinks and, inwards, dives again.

iii
    Back at the start
After the partial journey,
    His lack increased
By every landmark sighted,
    Poorer by far
Than at his first departure,
    He counts the lights
Indifferent eyes had charted,
    The lamps and stars
That leave him loss-benighted.

    A station built
Of soil's and sky's negation,
    An empty frame
Where grimy stillness strangles
    And shrill din stabs
Diminished meditation;
    In nerve and bone
Low tide of long delusion,
    Back at the start,
His partial destination.

iv
Night-flowering plant surprised, in memory
Her image grows complete. From root to flower –
Cool flame whose fire is water, earth and air –
His mind affirms her, darkness joined with day.

All one to Psyche, sunlight, lamp and moon
Shall not estrange her lover; well he knows
The tryst's illuminated mysteries
And knows, a diver proves no depth undone.

Bounded at last, his station waiting over,
He'll reach the relative streets and in them find
His landmarks all assembled, all contained,
Far light reflected in the central river.

Terrible still that city, but for love's
More vivid seasons: muffled the years rotate,

Lives intersect, their clash, their mergence mute,
And in their midst a hidden axle moves.

Based on its murderous rhythm music heals:
Tune, hands and mastered instrument reconciled
In silence, out of silence he can build
His personal architecture, sound its walls.

There – nymph a house for Psyche, flesh for ghost –
Within his monochrome fierce colours burn,
His glacier melts to moss and moss in turn
Suffers the transmutation of slow frost.

EMBLEM

Only for love of love
High up this hunter shot
And missed the snow-white dove;

Then, descending to the plain,
Entered a pitch-black wood
And, blindly, shot again.

For the sake of the dove, of mountain sunlight and snow
Deep in dark woods he seeks a wounded doe.

The links are chance, the chain is fate,
Constricting as Hephaistos' net
Which to the smiles of gods betrayed
Two bodies on a single bed,
So tightly knit, the truth was plain:
One multiplied by one is one.

Subtracting lovers who retort
That what chance coupled, choice can part
(As if mere effort could relax
The clutches of a paradox)
At last to their amazement find
Themselves the dwindled dividend,

Deep in that hell where Don Juan
Knows he has added names in vain
Since all the aggregate is lost
To him, not widowed but a ghost,
While those bereaved of one possess
A minus greater than his plus.

True love begins with algebra,
Those casual actors x and y,
Nonentities whose magic role
Is to turn nothing into all,
To be and not to be, to mate:
The links are chance, the chain is fate.

How I came to the place, I don't remember.
Like one on a pub-crawl in a foreign city,
Guided by those who know.

Suddenly I was there, deserted by all my guides,
Flung from a river-drifting drunkenness
Into those crowded confines, cruelly bright;
Sealed off from the city's flux and her stillness
As never in workshop, night-club or basement room,
Concert hall, prison or crypt.

Puzzled at first, seeing my look of pity,
They stared in silence: 'Who might this tourist be?
Angelic emissary? No. Nor simply spy.
One from the lukewarm regions rather, sent
By learned institute or university
To note our habits, tabulate our torment . . .
Out of his depth, has veiled his arrogant eye.'

So now they brawled and bawled, half deafened me,
Played leapfrog, squeezed and scratched their sores,
Fencing with red-hot pokers, scored by the scars
Their foils probed open, shrieked out the other's gain.
But at a sign from one lean inmate, ceased,
Rigid as he approached me:
                                        'Well, I'm blessed!
A temperate type dropped in on us,' he hissed.
'What's more, an anthropologist! –
No, don't deny it. Why, we're flattered.
I should have thought your welcome made that plain,
A warm, a rousing welcome, you'll admit.
And drop your bedside manner. We've no use for it.
No need to look pained. No need to look depressed.
A bit of a rough-house, eh? As if it mattered.
"Inhuman", did you mumble? Of all the rot! –
Enlighten the stranger. Tell him the answer, boys.'
In chorus they responded: 'We like noise!'
And then, fortissimo, 'We like it hot!'

As if to prove their freedom, unprompted they dispersed,
Each to his fire and intricate equipment.
A chemistry class, I thought, but saw no master;
And thought of cows come to the milking shed,
But missed the whacks and shouts.
                              Watching their work,
I moved around till nausea made me pause
Near one who held his left hand in the fire
And with the test-tube in his right hand scraped
The sizzling flesh away.
                        'Ah, yes, we burn,'
He answered when I questioned him, his glance,
Intent but calm, never once raised towards mine,
'With a hard gemlike flame. And in that urn –
No, not the refuse bin for trash the fire disdains,
That urn of pure white alabaster – place
The pure white ash, all that remains
After the ultimate metamorphosis
Of gross corporeal matter. This –
At once the end and product of my pains –
A messenger whose origin and identity
We lack the means to trace
Daily collects and – so I trust – delivers
Where the white lilies grow that feed on it.

'Sir, when you leave us, forget the coarse demeanour
By which the unsociable communicate,
Their play uproarious because their work is silent,
Their language lewd because their thought is rare.
Write of the lilies only – so white, so pure,
Our gaze could not endure them, who at best
Serve to enrich the soil of a garden for ever walled.'

Even while he spoke I saw his neighbour creep
Up to the pure white urn and shake its contents
Into a dust-pan, which in turn he emptied
Into the refuse bin.

Memory choked my protest.
'Thank you,' I gasped, 'thank you for every word.
I shall recall your candour and your trust

When in my mind the bloody wounds are blurred,
The din's an echo and even compassion numb.'
Then, longing for empty streets, I hurried out.

By twos and threes I climbed the dingy stairs,
Flung open the door and
                                    there,
A fond and faithful moll patiently waiting
Yet again at the prison gate,
Stood she who by the laughter smouldering in her eyes
Keeps lit the hellfire of my own undoing.

SEASON AND CIRCUMSTANCE

Sentence and Reply

i

Prison of circumstance, a foolproof sky,
Till death deliver him, shall bound his day
Who, blessed with folly, sheltered prudently,

Forsook his joy, to feel the rivers flow,
Put sheep to graze in meadows lush and low,
Lazed on the banks and watched his flock decay

With fat and foot-rot. Leave him to regret
The bordering hills might save them from their plight
Or else in sudden transit decimate

His weight of wealth who loved to travel light –
Living by skill in losing his estate –
Scorned name, relation, number . . . and would yet,

Could he but move. Make wind and waterfall,
Wingbeat of birds returning, cuckoo's call,
Ever more distant, taunt his dwindled will

And though with melted snow the river swell,
Flooding his land, let it be winter still
For him alone who once was mutable

But fearing death, turned traitor to the dead,
Bargained for time and shirked his proper trade,
Catastrophe, which now discomfited,

He longs to brave but cannot, his choice made.

ii
Love led me always. Love detains me now.
A one-way course, one river I follow,
Rushed with it shallow, deeper go slow.

The water feeds which brushed the rooted willow
To lay bare wood for the slow rain to kill
And with its rot replace eroded soil.

Restless in spring we travel, sooner to be still,
Dare out of fear what most we fear to know
And only plunge because afraid to fall;

More surely balanced, seem equivocal,
Past fear of falling, have no wish to climb,
Adept at nearly drowning, tempt no squall.

The sentence I approve, deny the crime:
Who serves a single season serves them all,
Serving the seasons never can serve time.

A pool I choose. It robs no waterfall,
Meshed with lush weeds would stop no rapid's flow.
I've crossed the hills that prove my pastures low

And here shall stay, unenvious of the swallow
Since moved or wintering always I have my will.
Spring wind and flood show best what stalks are hollow:

I'll cut no reeds and let the creepers grow.

'Soul, I protest. The shade of ancient trees,
The secret walks, walled garden and peacock's cry,
Dew on the lawns and the silence greater than these,
My heritage I gave up; and moved to the shanty town
That by subtraction of such properties,
Tethered to death and bare your peace I might own.
Soul, I protest. A dog's my conscience now.
His host and slave I rot in the hovel of pity,
Though with concrete, tin and plaster incessantly
I patch and build.'

     'Time's acre of mud you plough.

Why, false pedestrian, if now you're shamed
By a mere dog, anxiety,
Call on the fierce antagonists you tamed
When you were young to smother
That grovelling cur who will not let you be.
If your arm's feeble now, win peace by policy,
Pitting one devil against another.'

'You underrate the dog.
Pride and ambition, lust and cruelty
Will make a pact with him and pounce on me,
No less afraid to crush so loathed a creature
Than you to crush a spider or a frog.
In that half-animal
They sense the wild beast's fall,
Wolf, jackal, man all mingled in his nature.

'An obstinate lout can bend a stallion's will,
Stuck to his back until
Once centaur king they clear the thickest wall.
But if a cur snaps at the stallion's heels
A riven centaur reels
And in the ditch dog, horse and rider sprawl.

'Dog is the first to rise;
Then the great riderless horse who'll leap no more.
Still rigid, though unhurt, the rider lies,
Never once turning to forestall

Deeper and longer coma, his disgrace.
He does not stir before
A limping whimpering mongrel licks his face,
Fondly to stay with him. Long after he'll recall
That seal of love, the spittle on his eyes.

'Soul, set me free. In dreams I knock on the door
Of my own lost house, and they turn me away,
Fell the limes and the chestnuts, butcher the deer.
When I wake the dog's on my bed – and feeds on me,
Begs me to barter for a marrow-bone
The framed mementoes, ghosts of my possessions.
What next shall I renounce ?'

     'The lie
Of your renunciation that is none,
Crooked resort of the heart's lechery.

'Longer perhaps you should have lain
Dazed in the ditch; till you were whole
By virtue of that resting-place,
All memory of your horse and house,
Because a cur could love you, gone.

'Well there's another way – or more.
Whether you drag on crutches or
Fly for the joy of flying, where
Truly you are I too shall be.
Stylites' column, Xerxes' throne,
Neither is low, neither is high.
But you were gross in poverty.

'Dismiss the mongrel, then. Pick up
Your boots and spurs and riding-crop,
They'll do, if only you use them well,
Means to an end you guess. Now call
The horse that never could stray far,
You, his sole master after all,
Being so nearly motionless,
Get on your animal's back and ride
To the proud house the tall trees hide.'

EPITAPH FOR A HORSEMAN

Let no one mourn his mount, upholstered bone
He rode so cruelly over bog and stone,
Log, fence and ditch in every kind of weather;
Nor glibly hint those two came down together:
A horse fell dead and cast his master down,
But by that fall their union was undone.
A broken jade we found, the rider gone,
Leaving no token but his cold clean gear,
Bit, reins and riding-crop for friends to gather.
None but a beast's remains lie buried here.

III
Weather & Season
1958-1962

A tide, high tide of golden air.

Where, till this moment, were the bees?
And when no hum made for the honeysuckle,
Fumbled,
Became a body,
Clung and drank,
Spindrift, disowned, the petals hung,
And wait, let go was what the summer meant.

A corner of the garden, ivy on broken slats,
A branch with orange puffs: buddleia globosa.
Between two gusts a flood of golden air,
Mere hush, perhaps, abeyance – but the bees
Clinging and drinking.

Walls they brought with them: black courtyard in Paris,
A bit of marble, tumbled, dust on leaves,
A goldfish pond, the traffic not remote,
Audible, yet excluded;
Flowering tree or shrub in any weathered city,
Walls to contain a quietness, a quiver,
Fulfilment of the year, bees to be stilled.

Between two gusts, cold waves, the golden tide.

TIDES

To wake without fail when milk bottles shake in their racks,
Scrape one's face in the morning, every morning,
Take the same route to work and say 'good morning'
To the same row of scraped or powdered faces –
I cursed the roundness of this earth, I raged
At every self-perpetuating motion,
Hated the sea, that basher of dumb rock,
For all her factory of weeds and fishes,
The thumps, the thuds, the great reverberations —
Too much in rhythm; jarring, but by rote.

The metronome it was in my own head
That ticked and ticked; caged cricket in my head
That chirped and chirped until I had no ear
For syncopation, counterpoint of stillness
Beating against all music – of the sea,
Of birds and men, of season and machine,
Even of cricket and of metronome.
In silence I learned to listen; in the dark to look.

And unrepeatable now each morning's light
Modulates, shuffles, probes the daily faces
Often too suddenly different, like the street,
This weathered wall re-pointed, that new one cracked,
Apple trees that I prune while I forget
The shape of last year's boughs, cankered or grown,
And where that stump is, one that died in blossom;
Forget the hill's curve under the aerial masts.

No, wheels, grind on; seasons, repeat yourselves;
Milk bottles, rattle; familiars, gabble 'good morning';
Breed, hatch, digest your weeds and fishes, sea,
Omit no beat, nor rise to tidal waves.
Various enough the silences cut in
Between the rock cave's boom and the small wader's cry.

IN A CONVEX MIRROR

A stately room – chaise-longue and easy chairs,
Old jugs on carved commodes, a clavichord,
Three landscapes, minor eighteenth century,
Against the pale grey walls; and all in half-light,
The street being narrow, the houses opposite tall,
Each with a room like this – a waiting-room.

Sunk in a chair, quite still, a waiting man
Who stares into a classic composition
Heavily framed above the mantelpiece.
A streak of grey, myself in miniature
Against the pale pink upholstery, exhales
Invisible smoke; and slowly moves one hand,
Ten minutes only here, half lost already,
Half vanquished by the furniture, half absorbed,
But for the ticking of a clock would yield
All his defences, call the blur delusion.

But 'trumpery' now I mutter, jump up to break it,
Command my legs to walk, jerk my glazed eyes
Out of this glazed anachronism's eye,
And hear my name called; going, look once more;

A classic composition; nothing stirs.
One little streak of grey that matched the walls
Removed, but in that half-light far too faint
To leave a gap, and soon to be replaced.

THE BODY

Blue sky. White sand the wavelets lick and leave.
Alone his body struts, alone lies down.
Spiced with what springs, tautened in what tart winters,
It crouched and ran and leapt and climbed and hung,
Pulled at the oar, to exquisite horsebacks clung,
Rippled and swelled and sweated, flew on skis,
Braved currents, breakers, basked on how many shores.
The fruits and wines of every region fed it,
Beasts, wildfowl, fishes and more curious fauna
Its narrow bulk displaced. To the best winds it went,
Now noon, now morning sun for blending of its colour,
Now high, now low for cordials of good air.

None stalks it now to win or to admire,
Nor yet to kill. Of its own prime it dies
Where still he waits for her who in one glance will gather
Those foods, exertions, weathers, distances,
In his true landscape recognize her lover,
Each dear perfection answered in her eye.
Night took them all; smothers indifferently
Flesh of whatever tint, complexion, shape,
Abetting not the goddess but the woman,
Carnivorous mind more lithe than ever body was
In turning alien substances to gain;
Love, the sole acrobat, all limb and maw.

The sun's eye dims. No eye but his looks there.
A blotted contour, cold, his body struts
On greyish sand the wavelets lick and leave.

A HORSE'S EYE

I did not stop today at the five-barred gate,
Did not wait for the old white draught-horse at grass,
Unshod, unharnessed these many years; walked past,
Preoccupied, but something made me look back:
Her head was over the gate, her neck was straight,
But I caught her eye, a wicked, reproachful look
From one small eye slanted in my direction.
What right, I defied the old mare, what right had she
To expect caresses, the grass foolishly plucked
For her hanging lip, her yellow, broken teeth
And her great historical belly? Of course she's a relic,
Curious now as the old white country house
That stood empty and alluring in the wood behind her
Till converted into flats – not as useless as she,
Who will never become a tractor! What farmer would care?
Only some town-bred, animist, anthropomorphic rambler
Or week-end motorist looking for what he's lost.

I walked on; but plainly her glance had spoken to me,
As an old peasant's might in a foreign country,
Communicating neither words nor thought, but the knowledge
Of flesh that has suffered labour in rain and wind,
Fed, relaxed, enjoyed and opposed every season.
Broken now. Close to death. And how differently broken
From that Cossack mare the clumsiest rider could sit,
All speed and nerve and power that somehow responded
To the faintest twitch of a will less tense than her own!
Wild nature still; her eye no peasant's eye,
But lava under glass, tellurian fire contained.

As for the old white mare, her reproach was just:
Because she was too intelligible I had passed her by,
Because not alien enough, but broken as men are broken,
Because the old white house was converted now,
The wood about to be felled, a tractor chugging
Beyond the hill, and awkwardly she trotted
On legs too thin for her belly bloated with age,
Alone in her meadow, at grass, and close to death.

Whether dog will eat dog, likes boot leather frozen or boiled,
Whether walrus will prey on whale – the white or the grey ? –
Or only on seal – the bearded or common ? –
And is able in time to digest the clam swallowed whole;
Whether man can eat dog that has eaten the poisonous liver
Of polar bear, and wake up to indulge in a salad
Of sorrel and purple saxifrage after a breakfast of auks:
These were a few of the questions which if he did not answer
He probed as far as he could with his naked senses,
Knife-blade, bullet, harpoon, and the pain that probed him.
Fossils too he brought back and notes anthropologists noted –
The eskimo's fear not of narwhal but bumble bee –
Temperature charts and rough maps of the nameless mountains,
Cures for frostbite and skills never dreamed of at home,
Never called for either, never again to be used.

Brought back the knowledge that all his knowledge was loss;
And worse than loss, betrayal. Of musk-ox, of eiderduck?
Of gentle Eskimo, soon to be anyone's game?
Them and more. Of the hard land unlocked by his loving
To procure for the pimps of empire another whore.
And wished he had brought back nothing, not even his body,
Left it to wolf or to fox, to the poppies' ravenous roots
Or only glacier and silence, the diamond moonlight in winter.
Stayed there, died there in the first hard act.
Greater cold now he longed for, wider, more blizzard-swept skylines
For ever receding, crevasses more cunningly opening
And blindness, consummate vision, white, white to the point of blue,
Ice in his veins, and the snowlight burning to ice in his head.

BIRD WATCHER

Challenged, he'd say it was a mode of knowing –
As boys in railway stations neutralize a passion
By gathering ciphers: number, date and place –
Yet keeps no record of his rare encounters,
Darkly aware that like his opposite
Who no less deep in woods, as far out on the moors
Makes do with food and trophies, hunts for easy favours,
He trysts defeat by what he cannot know.

'Goldfinch' he says, and means a chirping flutter
From stalk to stalk in early autumn meadows,
Or 'oystercatcher', meaning a high, thin cry
More ghost than bodied voice, articulation
Of the last rock's complaint against the sea.

And wooing with his mind the winter fieldfares
Has made a snare of his binoculars,
For lime and cage and gun has longed in secret,
To kill that he may count, ravish despair
And eat the tongue that will not speak to him,
Though to the wind it speaks, evasive as the wind.

He grows no lighter, they no heavier
As to his mode of loving he returns,
Fixed in the discipline of adoration;
Will keep no pigeons, nor be satisfied
With metropolitan starlings garbling their parodies.

The boy's cold bride will yield, too soon and utterly,
Never these engines fuelled with warm blood,
Graced with peculiar folly that will far outfly him
Till in one communal emptiness they meet.

BLIND MAN

He can hear the owl's flight in daylight
When, surprised, on silky wings it shoots
From a low perch; and by the open window at night
The stag-beetles blundering in the hedges
On the far side of the meadow. Geese half a mile away
Honk near as hooters of swerving cars
And do not alarm him. Indifferently he awaits
Dogs that he feared when they slunk or bounded
Visible at him, as if in his carapace
Of darkness for ever secure from harm,
Wombed and housed and coffined within a wound
That has hardened to armour. The screech and the hum
Blend and subside in a resonant quiet,
Shapes he has fumbled to feel fall back
Into unbroken space when his hands forget them,
And still are present in his no man's land;
Above the nightmare tamed by light's extinction
The apple that hangs unplucked, grown fabulous.

Strange, but he cheats his master
Who without fail or stint pays in good notes and coinage,
For ever seeking to convert that currency
Into the sleep of metals and of stone.
Malachite, agate, lapis lazuli
Weigh down his papers; his eyelids are heavy with sleep.
Not bonds, not journals, line his inmost walls
But rows of books, his graveyard of choice minds,
Asleep until he rouses them,
Images fixed on paper, canvas, wood,
The discs engraved with voices of the dead,
Not flesh or leaf, time's pasture, but porcelain, ivory, bone.

Sleep is his wages; hatred of sleep
And fear of what might break it,
Sickness or slump,
The clumsy servant's duster,
Instruments of the retribution that will shatter
All that belies his means, outlasts his ends –
His master's ends, not his:
Though on a nightmare's back, he gallops into truth,
Though but to crash or stumble, rid of the glazed disasters
That were his juggler's toys,
Feel the raw grain and jagged crust of earth
And wake to serve his master loyally.

CONFORMIST

Branded in childhood, for thirty years he strove
To hide the scar, and truly to believe
In the true fundaments of that commonweal
Which once had outlawed him beyond repeal,
And with true awe, true gratitude, true love
Would gaze upon the incorruptible guard
Before the gate – the keeper of his peace
Who in mean streets could live anonymous . . .

Until conformity brought its reward:
A crested, gilt-edged card. The great gate opened,
A pair of stiff lips cracked and let him pass
Into those halls his half life's dreams had deepened;

And out again . . . to breathe the ownerless air,
Night sky transfigured, lucent fresh and clear
After the ceilings puffed in emulation.
His own place found at last; his own self found –
Outside, outside – his heritage regained
By grace of exile, of expropriation.

What had he seen, ushered behind the gate?
The dress and furniture of his own terrors,
A glittering medal pinned on his own wound,
And, at the heart, an empty hall of mirrors.

Healed now, of health, unmasked, of honesty,
In, out again he passed, with one smile met
The questioning eyes of flunkey, potentate,
Townsman and guard shrunk to complicity,

All one to him at one with every station
Since none was his, nor ever now could be;
Come late into the freedom his from birth,
To breathe the air, and walk the ownerless earth.

Trunk hard and ridged, more fit for hedges
If more than trunk, not by a curious marriage
Disarmed of spikes, lopped and tamed in an orchard
To bear this wealth of delicate boughs cascading,
Flounced pink, downed gold, devoured by parasites
Strange to his grain's potential, fostered disapproving.

Crest lithe and light, the weather's dancer
But for the bitter moods for ever rising
From his dark roots and the dank clay beneath;
Fearing each leaf-fall, fruit-fall, yearly diminished
Not for his sake, to swell the festering humus
That breeds and buries, feeds and chokes unheeding.

Gardener indeed, who grafted quince on hawthorn,
Binding two kinds, two minds, by one sap mellowed,
Lifelong divided, indivisible lifelong in labour
For fruit not like the suns's gold or his aborted berries,
Gratuitous, never learned the art of undoing,
From wounded fibre exacts the blossom whole!

Trunk hard and ridged, more fit for hedges
But for his wealth, her delicate boughs cascading
From his dark roots and the dank clay beneath;
By dint of wealth, downed gold by one sap mellowed,
Grown more than trunk or his aborted berries:
Crest lithe and light, the weather's dancer.

THE MOMENT

Trapped in the whorls of a conch time roared.
Eye, mind met walls,
Could neither enter nor rebound,
The moment lost in plotting for the act.

Sleep cracked the shell,
In lidded eyes unlocked the cells of light,
Undid no knot long fingered,
Traced no new shape, nor any sign but this:

Morning, the slanted beams
Through low dark boughs and the bunched leaves of bushes.
A streak of lawn illuminated? Yet
It was not grass or grain of wood and leaf
That held the moment whole. It was the angle:
Sunlight, and how it fell.

INSTEAD OF A JOURNEY

Turn like a top; spin on your dusty axis
Till the bright metal shines again, your head
Hums and the earth accelerates,
Dizzy you drop
Into this easy chair you drowse in daily.
Sit there and watch the walls assume their meaning,
The Chinese plate assert its blue design,
The room renew itself as you grow still.
Then, after your flight and fall, walk to the garden
Or at the open window taste return:
Weather and season, clouds at your vision's rim,
Love's whims, love's habitation, and the heart
By one slow wheel worn down, whetted to gladness.

IV
Observations & Ironies
1959-1969

> *Yesterday, just before being transported*
> *back to prison, I committed a terrible*
> *gaffe. Two people came out of the inter-*
> *rogation room. One of them, tall, elegant,*
> *speaking a very cultivated French, looked*
> *so tormented, as though about to break*
> *down. I asked him with concern: 'Vous*
> *ont-ils malmené?' 'Qui ça?' 'Mais eux.'*
> *He looked at me, shrugged his shoulders*
> *and walked on. Then the German sentry said:*
> *'But that's a Gestapo man.'*
>   Prison Diary of E. A. Rheinhardt,
>   *Nice, Jan. 22nd 1944.*

Later, back in my cell, back in the thick stench
From the bucket shared with three men whose dreams are of flesh
Not for beating or fondling but eating, I laugh, laugh
As never before in that place, even when gorged with a treat
Of gift food from a parcel. For then I would drift
Away from our common attrition by hunger and filth
To my garden, those hardly believable flowers
That may open again though I am not there to tend them,
To my bed and, almost, the mingling of bodies in lust,
And would hate the voice that clattered into my refuge
With a curse or a joke. Now they are close to me,
My fellow victims, decent men at the most,
Blundering into death as I do, devoid of a fury to hurl
Against our tormentors, the furious burners of books
Numb with the icy need to know nothing, be strong.
I laugh, laugh at their strength, at our feebleness
And laughing feel how one I could not believe in
Allows me to blaze like his martyrs, consumes me
With love, with compassion; and how the soul
Anatomists cannot locate even now will rise up
When my turn comes to blunder again, when I cry
To the killer who cracks my joints: 'Je te comprends, mon ami . . .'

TREBLINKA

A Survivor Speaks:

That winter night they were burning corpses
And from the bonfire, flooding the whole camp
Flared purple and blue and red and orange and gold,
The many colours of Joseph's coat, who was chosen.
Not cold for once we at the barrack windows
Blinked and listened; the opera singer,
Unafraid for once, found his full voice and gave it
To words, to a music that gushed like blood from a wound:
Eli, Eli . . . his question too in whose name
Long we'd been dirt to be wiped off, dust to be dispersed –
Older than he, old as the silence of God.
In that light we knew it; and the complaint was praise,
Was thankfulness for death, the lost and the promised land,
The gathering up at last, all our hundred hues
Fierce in one radiance gathered by greater darkness,
The darkness that took our kings, David and Solomon
Who living had burnt with the same fire;
All our hundred languages gathered again in one silence.

To live was the law; though to live – and not only here –
Was a hundred times over to spit in our own faces,
Wipe ourselves out of creation, scatter as dust,
Eat grass, and the dung that feeds grass.
The grass, the dung, the spittle – here we saw them consumed,
Even these bodies fit in the end to yield light.

Back in a room in a house in a street in a town
I forget the figures, remember little but this:
That to live is not good enough: everything, anything
Proved good enough for life – there, and not only there.
Yet we lived, a few of us, perhaps with no need but this:
To tell of the fire in the night and briefly flare like the dead.

IN A COLD SEASON

i
Words cannot reach him in his prison of words
Whose words killed men because those men were words
Women and children who to him were numbers
And still are numbers though reiterated
Launched into air to circle out of hearing
And drop unseen, their metal shells not broken.
Words cannot reach him though I spend more words
On words reporting words reiterated
When in his cage of words he answered words
That told how with his words he murdered men
Women and children who were words and numbers
And he remembered or could not remember
The words and numbers they reiterated
To trap in words the man who killed with words.
Words cannot reach the children, women, men
Who were not words or numbers till they died
Because ice-packed in terror shrunk minds clung
To numbers words that did not sob or whimper
As children do when packed in trucks to die
That did not die two deaths as mothers do
Who see their children packed in trucks to die.

ii
Yet, Muse of the IN-trays, OUT-trays,
Shall he be left uncelebrated
For lack of resonant numbers calculated
To denote your hero, and our abstract age?
Rather in the appropriate vocabulary
Let a memorandum now be drawn up –
Carbon copies to all whom it may concern –
A monument in kind, a testimonial
To be filed for further reference
And to circulate as required.
Adolf Eichmann, civil servant (retired):
A mild man, meticulous in his ways,
As distinctly averse to violence
As to all other irregularities

Perpetrated in his presence,
Rudeness of speech or deportment,
Infringements of etiquette
Or downright incompetence, the gravest offence;
With a head for figures, a stable family life,
No abnormalities.
Never lost his temper on duty
Even with subordinates, even with elements earmarked
For liquidation;
Never once guilty of exceeding his authority
But careful always to confine his ambitions
Within the limits laid down for personnel of his grade.
Never, of course, a maker of policy,
But in its implementation at office level,
Down to the detailed directive, completely reliable;
Never, perhaps, indispensable,
Yet difficult to replace
Once he had mastered the formalities
Of his particular department
And familiarized himself with his responsibilities
As a specialist in the organization
Of the transport and disposal of human material –
In short, an exemplary career.

iii
Words words his words – and half his truth perhaps
If blinking, numb in moonlight and astray
A man can map the landmarks trace the shapes
That may be mountains icebergs or his tears
And he whose only zeal was to convert
Real women children men to words and numbers
Added to be subtracted leaving nothing
But aggregates and multiples of nothing
Can know what made him adept in not knowing
Feel what it was he could not would not feel –
And caged in words between their death his death
No place no time for memory to unfreeze
The single face that would bely his words
The single cry that proved his numbers wrong.

Probing his words with their words my words fail.
Cold cold with words I cannot break the shell
And almost dare not lest his whole truth be
To have no core but unreality.

iv
I heard no cry, nor saw her dying face,
Have never known the place, the day,
Whether by bullet, gas or deprivation
They finished her off who was old and ill enough
To die before long in her own good time;
Only that when they came to march her out of her human world,
Creaking leather couch, mementoes, widow's urn,
They made her write a postcard to her son in England.
'Am going on a journey'; and that all those years
She had refused to travel even to save her life.
Too little I know of her life, her death,
Forget my last visit to her at the age of nine,
The goodbye like any other that was the last,
Only recall that she, mother of five, grandmother,
Freely could share with a child all her little realm;
Recall her lapdog who trembled and snapped up cheese –
Did they kill her lapdog also, or drive him away? –
And the bigger dog before that, a French bulldog, stuffed
To keep her company still after his early death.
Three goldfishes I recall, one with a hump on his back
That lived for years though daily she brushed her fishes
Under the kitchen tap to keep them healthy and clean:
And how she conspired with us children,
Bribed us with sweets if we promised not to tell
Our father that she, who was diabetic,
Kept a pillbox of sweets in her handbag
To eat like a child in secret –
When neither could guess that sweets would not cause her death.
A wireless set with earphones was part of the magic
She commanded and freely dispensed,
Being childlike herself and guileless and wise . . .

Too little I know of her wisdom, her life,
Only that, guileless, she died deprived
Of her lapdog even, stuffed bulldog and pillbox of sweets.

V

And yet and yet I would not have him die
Caged in his words their words – one deadly word
Setting the seal on unreality
Adding one number to the millions dead
Substracting nothing from death dividing nothing
Silencing him who murdered words with words
Not one shell broken, not one word made flesh.
Nor in my hatred would imprison him
Who never free in fear and hatred served
Another's hatred which again was fear
So little life in him he dared not pity
Or if he pitied dared not act on pity;
But show him pity now for pity's sake
And for their sake who died for lack of pity;
Break from the husk at last one naked grain
That still may grow where the massed carrion lay
Bones piled on bones their only mourners bones
The inconceivable aggregate of the dead
Beyond all power to mourn or to avenge;
See man in him spare woman child in him
Though in the end he neither saw nor spared –
Peel off the husk for once and heed the grain,
Plant it though he sowed nothing poisoned growth;
Dare break one word and words may yet be whole.

BECAUSE

To the child's 'why?' parents invent an answer,
To adult man's, scientist and philosopher
Their long cacophonous chorus of 'because'.
How mind abhors a circle! Let there be laws!
A schoolboy knows effects must have a cause.
All know it but the wise man and the dancer,
Tautologists who as they turn are still,
Find every virtue in a vicious circle –
The serpent's mouth that bites the serpent's tail –
And are because they are because they are.

SOLIDARITY

There's honour among thieves, both in and out of prison,
Fellowship even, in the teeth of competition,
And sorority among whores – though mainly off-duty,
On sea-side vacations, or after the ruin of beauty –
But strongest and strangest of all is the solidarity
Of respectable men in respectable company.
Would it be drink that does it? Dissolving differences,
Discrete achievements and individual purities?
No, they feel it when sober, not only at parties and luncheons,
But in boardrooms, common rooms, barracks, or charging with truncheons.
It comes over them suddenly – not a warm, not a vernal breath,
Yet kindling warmth in cold hearts – the bad conscience of death,
Communist at the frontier bound in time to break through,
But, teacher of love among convicts, Christian too.

WORDS

'A writer you call yourself? And sit there tongue-tied
While others talk about books?
Jolted, answer in monosyllables, non-committal at that.
Are you shy, then, or sly? Superior or plain dim-witted?
Do we bore you or aren't you there?'

'A bit of all these. But words are the root of the trouble.
Because I can't speak – what I can't speak – I write.
Words? Yes, words, I can't do without them.
But I hate them as lovers hate them
When it's time for bodies to speak;
As an acrobat would,
Asked to tell how he leaps, why he leaps, when he's leaping.
A curious trade, I admit:
Turning a thing into words so that words will render the thing;
Setting a movement to words so that words will render the movement.
But words about words about things? I can do without them.
Look: the arc-lamp's game with the plane-tree's windblown branches.
Listen: an owl. And those voices – closing time down the street.
And smell: the coffee boiled over two minutes ago.'

LIFE AND ART I

For Denis Lowson

'A cell,' I reply when visitors remark
On the small high windows of the room I work in,
A room without a view. 'Exactly what I need,
Daylight enough – no more – to push a pen by,
And no distractions. Even the two great elms
With their congregations, race riots and social conflicts,
Endless commotion of squirrels, jackdaws and owls
Not to be seen, and only seldom heard.'

You dropped in one morning and sketched the garden,
All blue and black with the bulk and shade of those elms.
At once I longed to possess it (The garden, the sketch ?)
And above my desk I pinned up the silence extracted
From the endless commotion of squirrels, jackdaws and owls.
My garden hangs on the wall – and no distractions.

LIFE AND ART II

Because I was writing my poem on sticklebacks –
Day in, day out, again and again
Till I scrapped it, tore up all the drafts –
I forgot to feed them. Mere babies, they gobbled up
Every unarmoured, toothless and spikeless creature
Left alive in the tank –
Tinier still they'd picked off
The fry of fishes potentially four times their size –
To the last food grain competed for Lebensraum,
Then weakened and died.

I loved them, of course,
(Inhumani nihil etc. – as long as it's nature:
Frogs collide with toads in my creepery garden)
Their fins always aquiver,
Their mottled mackerel sheen,
How they shot, torpedoes in search of ships –
And was full of remorse.
I'd been waiting to see the males
Flush carmine, magnesium blue in the breeding season,
Bravely defend their nests.

Yet my conscience took comfort, too, at the thought:
One love poem less.

EROS

Big shot ? Bad shot. Bungler.
With a fine arrowhead pierces
The wrong breast,
Lets a blunt one
Bounce off the right.
Arrested. For ever a kid.

CRISE DE FOIE

> *'As for serving, our livers will do that*
> *for us.'*
>> Adam, Head Waiter at the *Wild Isle*

And did they ? In their lifetime pickled,
Living it up ? When revolution came,
Non serviam on every manjack's bib,
Lords of your kidney drew long faces
And, galled by common fare, lost heart.
A Finnish soup, Sibelius
Too soon ran out. No other course remained.
The white-gloved Maître, the finnicky Chef
Mopped the last plates and scrubbed the floor.

VEHICLES

But you preferred my 'one' and 'he' and 'we'?
My reticence? Humility? Liked me more
When wrapped in myth and mask and metaphor
I kept my beasts heraldic, men heroic,
Rhythm and stanza tidy, bearing stoic?
Before, a blabber, I loosed 'the odious me'?

Humble? I cared for it, I made a fuss
Of that indifferent, second-hand machine,
(It looked as good as new), for ever busy
Maintaining, patching up my poor tin lizzy,
So anxious that to keep the panels clean
And spare the engine I would go by bus.

And now? I like it more and less
All scraped and dented, in a mess,
My boneshaker that still keeps going.
It's past re-chroming now, re-spraying,
Past washing too. And so I let.
The garage, park it in the street.
I cannot sell it, cannot lose it,
Can neither spoil it nor misuse it
Though far I drive it, drive it hard,
Knowing that in the breaker's yard
Something will last, perhaps to move
What singular and plural cove –
But not the paintwork, not the chrome:
No car of mine will drive me home.

SICK TRANSIT

Gloria Mundy, the fashion model,
Hand on hip, steps
From the Paris–London 'plane,
Her luggage this autumn's inanity
Carried with blank poise
From blank face to
Blank face;
From bank to bank.

IN PHILISTIA

Thoughts after a public reading
of new verse

'To affirm the affirmative'. Yes.
With a lean or a fat smirk
To confirm: that's how we are, human.
Not to shirk nappies,
Knowingly to acknowledge
I know what you know:
That people may laugh or vomit
In face of their dead,
Lovers may bore each other,
The bomb is the bomb.

Tedious economy:
Those pennies they drop in our hats
We spin or jingle for them,
They thank us for showing them pennies.

Not sapiens, though, but quaerens
(Excuse the presumption of Latin)
They walk when we are not looking.
We walk when oblivious of them.

MAL D'AUTRUI

She comes, my headache, my bellyache,
My toothache, to torment me,
With moist, with mad eyes
That mean no harm, so full
Of her luxurious grieving
Their nature is not to see –
Geysers of other-pain
In whose hot vapours I gasp,
They scald me with their gushing
Till, cold, I shrink away.

Unfeeling? Murderous now
With pity that she disdained
Who swore to kill herself
And punish the world for not caring,
I care too much to be cruel,
Too little now to implore:
My headache, bellyache, toothache,
Worse than all these, outside me,
Despair of dentist and doctor,
Forgive me for not being you.

The newspaper in my hands
Reports a four-sided battle
In the streets of a town
I shall never see.
What I see, what I read
Will depend on this war,
The sum and ratio of men
Maimed or killed on each side.

The newspaper in my hands
Omits to count the losses.
On a fifth side – the people.
Yet the winner, if any, will count
The people, if any, left over
Because with no people to rule
The winners would not be the winners,
The war itself would not count.

The newspaper in my hands
Will serve to light a fire,
Yesterday's casualties burn
On my grate tomorrow
Or perhaps with dead leaves in the garden;
Tomorrow's newspaper bring me
Headlines that cancel out
Yesterday's interim score.

The newspaper in my hands
Begins to smoulder, to stink
As I read the day's gossip
About business and fashion,
Parties and mergers and
This gossip-monger's views
On a news handout on
A book on a fashion-pimp.

The newspaper in my hands
Begins to rot my hands.
I drop the newspaper, stare:
From my right forefinger
Something obtrudes. I pinch it.
And pull out a worm, then another.

I look at my left hand:
Hollowed out, a black stump.
Amid all those woodlice
Scurrying there I spot
A big slug. With a matchstick held
Between worm-eaten fingers
I spear the slug, remove it.
And nothing hurts. Nothing.

CREDO

Some argue that the universe is expanding.
We know it's expendable.
Others argue that the universe is contracting.
We know it's contracted for.
Put a parking lot on Mars
And folks will go there, forget about breathing.
Put a supermarket on Venus
And it's ripe for development.
Let the universe shrink or bust:
Civilization – and that means us –
Will keep moving from deal to deal.

Looks for its body among
The skyscrapers, tenement blocks
Where a white man's unwise to walk.
At the thought of revolution
Sends kites, balloons into air opaque
With excremental vapours of produce
And sees them vanish, glad
That where they've gone they'll be free.
Meanwhile it feeds refrigerators
With bags of lobster tails, whole sides of prime beef,
Homogenized milk by the gallon; and, hailed by Donuts,
By Steak or Chicken Dinner it glides
Down Main Street emptily, starving
For the smell of newly baked bread.

In the beginning was business. But the facts are obscure
Because no accounts were kept and even the Founder's person
Is veiled in mystery. All we know is the rules
Passed on to the management by one of such absolute power,
So revered and so rarely seen that even to speak his name
Was a deadly offence. And who can deny that a residue
Of that primal awe still adheres to the policy-making
Heads of corporations, whatever the system and ownership?
Our six-day week (where not yet reduced to five)
Goes back to that mythical phase and the rules laid down
By the Father of Commerce. Likewise from earliest records
We learn how this Earth with its minerals, flora and fauna
And finally Man, was created – needless to say
As material for business, which was in the beginning,
Though we also read of the Word (or Logos), the medium
Which more than any other human attributes, even including
Our manual skill and inventiveness, furthered the progress
Of business from primitive barter to modern finance.
For words and numbers permitted the gradual transition
From chattel to coin and lastly paper economies.
This is called evolution: the origin of species =
('A particular sort of coin or money. Coinage, coin,
Money, bullion. Metal used for coinage.' Oxford English Dictionary)
Is the key to history proper. And words mark the turning-points,
As when somebody, doubtless a man of genius,
Coined this figure of speech, 'The Shop of State',
Showing sudden total awareness of that which distinguishes
Our highly developed nation states from all that had gone before,
Or when Napoleon called England 'a nation of shopkeepers',
A description at that time construed as less than a compliment,
Although it was more, a prophecy based on the recognition
Of how the Industrial Revolution had changed the structure
Of one great nation, as later it must every other's
Regardless of whether its products and prices and rate of investment
Were controlled by cartel, competition or state monopoly.

So much for history. Henceforth we may take it for granted
That the cosmos itself and human life on this planet

With its institutions and enterprises, organizations and laws
Has, and was meant to have, only one ultimate end,
The growth and perfection of business, of wealth and of power.
It remains to clear up a number of seeming complexities,
Conflicts and contradictions. E.g. a few men and women
Have been heard to grumble like this: 'A consumer society?
Haven't people always consumed? And isn't the point about ours
That we have to consume whatever is put on the market,
Not what *we* want? A producer society, then,
It ought to be called.' Well, apart from the quibble,
That objection condemns the objector as one with no proper concern
In the shop of state; a misfit, parasite, dropout
Whom psycho-ideological tests will invariably prove
To harbour an atavistic, anti-historical, irreligious
Craving for simple 'things' – a form of regression
No civilized order can tolerate, the point about ours
Being that it rests not on 'things' but on tokens
Or symbols – like money, commodities, words.
The very same truth confutes the subversive chatter of those
Who charge our world with 'materialism'. A world in which matter
Has ceased to matter – can that be materialistic?
It's the token, the symbol that counts. Which brings us back
To where we began – to the mystery.
Our shopkeepers, up to the hierarchies
Of Presidents, Chairmen, Prime Managers, may forget
What ancient flame they are guardians of, what holy office they serve,
What authority, vested in them, they administer.
Yet, rightly, we praise and adore them and fear their might.
So be it, then; as it was in the beginning
And ever shall be, except for improvements,
Inevitable adjustments, fluctuations in currency values.

LINES DISCOVERED IN A LONDON DUSTBIN

North Kensington

Hung up on true love and all that jazz
I looked for a woman among
the miniskirts miniminds maxipresumptions
and found combinations of
sex and pot pot and drink drink and sex
mixed and offered like cocktails
with male and female organs
now here now there so that in the end I wondered
to whom they belonged.
My conclusion was: no one.
Thrill computers about as predictable
as those moon mites packed into capsules
to infest with multiple gadgets
the virginal pale one who long
by remote control had ruled
the lunatic the lover and the poet.
Amplified emptiness deafened me.
I starved in a world full of feedback.

Retrogressive I turned to terrestrial nature
and all that jazz –
O Woods O Fountains Hillocks Dales and Bowrs –
only to read in the papers
that two Belgian microbiologists
had abolished nature, inducing a symbiosis
of plants with bacteria,
laboratory marriages that would lead
to unheard-of mutations
and establish man as the ultimate manipulator
of so-called entelechy, his own included.
Maybe, maybe not. There was always the bomb
another agent of change. But either way it seemed likely
that one day nothing more would remain on this earth
to be botched. And that was enough to make me apologize
to animals plants bacteria
for having taken their names in vain.
I received an answer: excommunication.

There was always the bomb. And protest.
Duly I had protested –
quite lately against the imprisonment
by a right-wing dictatorship
of a left-wing intellectual
whose last public gesture before the event
had been to protest against the protest
occasioned by the imprisonment
by a left-wing dictatorship
of two left-wing intellectuals
who disliked dictatorships.
This made it necessary to protest
that I had protested not in favour of the protest
against the protest but only
against the imprisonment; and that in future
I should feel it incumbent on me to protest
against protests against the protests
of those who protested as I had done
against the imprisonment of protesters.
But the good resolution
proved too much even for bad verse:
blue in the face with impossible contortions
my muse fell dead, strangled by her own arms.
Her last words were a protest: protest and all that jazz . . .

Well, I could have cashed in on the lady's demise,
rid at last of a troublesome accessory
long outmoded in any case, expensive to keep up,
an extravagance really now that surrogates
are a drug on the market, posters
count more than poems and gossip columns
have replaced immortality. All that was needed
for a new career was to make myself useful
to the dealers in fame fashion fun,
becoming a personality – if only it weren't
for something perverse in me that prefers
to be cold clean unremarkable
dust or ash, which cannot be sold.
In short I'm packing it up, going
underground for good, defecting
to the other side. And promptly too,

before the social planners install
death-wish detectors in every home,
with powers to impose the life penalty
for so much as a day-dream of crossing the border.
I leave no advice no property
and no poems. Only these posthumous lines.

V
Dream Poems
1961-1972

THE ROAD

It begins near Venice,
A Venice of chasms and pools,
And above a coastline longer than vision
Gently curves
Into a south or east without end.
Always the question is
How far can I walk it
Across what frontiers
Into what vastnesses,
More golden mist,
Woods even denser, darker,
Mountains more mountainous
Above a more dazzling sea.

Always I am detained;
As by this new nation
Of displaced persons
Who are rarely visited,
Whose nationhood is a cause.
They needed me,
Appealed to my fellowship,
Involved me in schemes,
Charged me with missions
To friends whom I never reached.

If only I could move on
To the wilder, more alien countries
Further along the road.

THE SEARCH

As commanded, I looked for my origin,
Passed through the town in which my grandfather settled
And found no street that I knew;
On through the suburbs, blind bungalows,
Lilac, laburnum, narrowly flowering
And out into mountains, woods,
Far provinces, infinities of green.
Walked, walked, by day, by night,
Always sure of the route
Though the people grew foreign, bizarre;
And the birds, a species unheard of, remembered me.
At last I came to a village
Where they told me: here you were born.
An unlikely place – no petrol pump, office block, poster? –
Yet I could not deny it, and asked them the name:
Why, Mors, need we tell you, m o r s, MORS.

SCENARIO

i
He came home. Came home? The house
Did not fit the garden, the view.
Their own, locked up in his absence?
Another she'd bought and unlocked?
On the floor of a half-lit room
Lay family silver, baskets full,
Tapestries, paintings he could not remember possessing,
A screen of beaten brass,
Concertina of Indian dancers,
Flimsy, garish, in half-relief,
All dumped there to be discarded
Or, if he chose, kept to furnish the house.

ii
Threading his way to the garden through crowds of guests
He looked for his landmarks and frontiers:
To the north a great railway station
Linked to the house by a concrete road
That brought more guests in taxis.
To the south a valley and, hazily shining,
Cupolas, palace roofs, towers
Framed in mountain-tops, wooded ravines.

A woman stood near him, a stranger.
'Lend me your eyes,' he begged her, 'I mean,
Tell me, describe what *you* see.
My left eye fear, my right eye desire
Will not focus; all shifts and blurs.
Where am I?' She laughed, and moved on.

iii
Room after room. Bare galleries, halls,
Passages, thronged with guests.
Unrecognized he explored them,
Came to an improvised kitchen
And found his wife with a man.
'Hallo!' she said, and smoothed her lover's hair.

He turned on his heel, strode through the staring crowds
And, alone in the garden, waited.
They followed: a burly man,
A fence between them. He vaulted,
The man seized his leg, pulled him down,
Hurled a knife, then a pitchfork,
But felled by his fists, lay still.

The single boom of a gong.

iv
Longer than sight the table stretched,
Between bare walls without end,
Faces, faces, to each of which now with an effort
He could have attached a name, a function, a place.
'So the three of you will be living together'
Neighed the sleek-haired one with a bow tie.
'It's hard enough to live with one's wife,
Let alone her lover' he heard himself answer.
A *bon mot*, apparently. Between their guffaws
He corrected himself: 'But no reflection
On *my* wife. A general observation.'
Had she heard him? He did not know where she was.

v
He walked with her and their only child, a daughter,
No house in sight, no intruder,
The three of them anywhere, walking in silence.
He turned to her: 'Is it true . . .?'
Needing her confirmation of the silence
That made her true again, gathered into a moment
Their moments and years.
'Quiet' she said, 'not now – the child'.
And knifeblade, pitchfork went home,
Pierced him with love, the first and the last pain.

FOR NO ONE

So we meet again, little girl
Whose blue eyes taught me
How to say nothing, to look
And be merged in looking.
I saw you there and I listened,
But you cannot hear me,
Nor do I know where you are.
No need, in that place
Where to look is enough,
Where to meet is a marriage
Nowhere, for ever,
Nothing can be undone.

Here, I should have passed by, unrecognizing,
You a woman now, still young but not beautiful
With a bad complexion. But Beatrice was your name,
Recalled me without words though your eyes were not even blue
And now you chattered gaily about yourself,
About living from hand to mouth, luxuriously.
Because you were Beatrice, nothing had changed between us;
Because nothing had changed between us, I knew your name.

'I fell asleep in a flowering meadow:
Steely light, high up, was honing the swallows' wings.

'I woke when dry twigs rattled,
Scratching the brickwork, a street lamp yellowed the wall.

'Where have I been? Where am I? Flung like a stone
Through the days and weeks, late summer and autumn.'

'You were ill,' she said, 'and now you are better,
Your weathers, your streams and your hills, they're all in your head.

'On a welded frame you were born. Under a ceiling of plaster.
No bird flew there. Not even a bluebottle buzzed

'On the clean glass. No bud broke from table or chair.
Heat was turned on, turned off. Like the light, the water.

'Your children, look, have grown strong in their human seasons,
Content but for you. Waiting for you to come back.'

'Back. Yank me back, then, through thunder and blizzards.
Blundering, wandering, blind in the rain, in the sun.

'Black I was. Blacked out. Looking for blackberries, nuts,
In rooms painted white. And losing the flowers in my head.

'The crazy daisies. The comatose roses. The funny honeysuckle.
Made in Noland for no one. No sooner seen than gone.

'Give me time. Convince me that your time is mine.
Make me tick as the clock ticks – till the clock runs down.

'Hold me, hold me, I'm falling. The swallows freeze in mid-air.
They've ploughed my meadow. The trees are bare.'

MEMORY

My wives do not write.
Sweetly young, hair flowing,
They walk where they belong,
Riverside, lakeside,
Mountainside, hillside,
Woodland or grassy plain.

One I consoled –
Black-haired, sad
In her forest clearing –
Another I followed
From a wellspring up in the scree
To a pool's golden rushes.

Did I leave them, forsake them?
I travelled,
Remember no parting.
Ways, I recall, transitions,
The shadows, the colours turning,
Herbs acrid or heady,
Sweet wives the world over,
Sweet virgins walking where they belong –

Unchanged, unchanging regions,
And they unchanged.

But by the knee a stranger
Clawed me, held on;
I fought: my grappling hand
Slid deep into rotten flesh,
A hole behind his ear.
I knocked him down and ran,
Clegs covering me,
A grey crust;
Ran to the church, thinking
They could not enter there,
But still they clung, stinging,
And up I climbed, climbed
To the belfry, pursued
By a man half-decayed.

Sweet wives, sweet virgins
Walk still unchanged,
Do not write, do not miss me,
Never forget.
It was the sunshine, the shadows,
It was the herbs and the haze.

THEOGONY

One feather, scarlet, on snow:
High rose the bird
That feeds by winter moonlight,
Warbles on farthest mountain tops,
By no man snared, by no man plucked or eaten.

One golden hair
Found on the pillow:
The woman gone, Diana of all that was hers
Grazes with absence the tiled floor
And hallows it, touched by her feet once.

THE BLIGHT

Somewhere behind us, from the long room,
Sear-frost, look! cried a child's voice
As fingertips touching we stood
At the window and looked,
Felt the sap run again
From the root up,
New boughs burgeon under the new sun.

Sere-frost, in April?
There it was, icy rain,
And the leaves turned black, curled,
Bud, blossom shrivelled, fell,
Not one year's growth but the whole tree withered.

Your hand froze in mine,
Froze mine, yet tightened, the nails
Dug in through flesh drained numb,
Dug down to the bones and a deep nerve.

Let go, if you can.

Too slowly toward the root
Our death creeps.

BY THE SEA

For weeks now
In coves, in the deeper dips
Of the dunes, in cave mouths,
Daily almost, a corpse has been found,
Of a man, young or aging,
Of a boy. Mangled.
The cause of death?
Drowned, says one report,
Another, strangled.
Never afloat. Never bloated.

Called upon to investigate
I combed the coast, came
To this rocky beach, saw
A line of bodies laid out,
Five, a green film
Covering each. Halted there,
On the low cliff, gaped,
Unable to move.
But one of them
Moved.
Slithered on to the next
And dug in, with nails,
Lips, teeth, gulping.

I yelled, yelled for a rifle to kill
The carnivore. Who sleek
As a seal, but
Girl-waisted now, girl
Breasts, girl buttocks
Outlined under the green
Slime, wriggled
Quickly toward the water,
Rippled away, merged.

VI
Of Time & Place
1961-1967

SECURITY

i

So he's got there at last, been received as a partner –
In a firm going bankrupt;
Found the right place (walled garden), arranged for a mortgage –
But they're pulling the house down
To make room for traffic.

Worse winds are rising. He takes out new policies
For his furniture, for his life,
At a higher premium
Against more limited risks.

ii

Who can face the winds, till the panes crack in their frames?
And if a man faced them, what in the end could he do
But look for shelter like all the rest?
The winds too are afraid, and blow from fear.

iii

I hear my children at play
And recall that one branch of the elm-tree looks dead;
Also that twenty years ago now I could have been parchment
Cured and stretched for a lampshade,
Who now have children, a lampshade
And the fear of those winds.
I saw off the elm-tree branch
To find that the wood was sound;
Mend the fences yet again,
Knowing they'll keep out no one,
Let alone the winds.
For still my children play,
And shall tomorrow, if the weather holds.

OMENS

i

The year opens with frozen pipes,
Roads impassable, cars immovable,
Letter delivery slow;
But smallpox from Pakistan
Carried fast from Yorkshire to Surrey,
And no lack of news:
In the Andes a landslide
That buried a town;
In Dalmatia, earthquakes;
Bush fires around Melbourne,
Cooking wallabies, koala bears.
In the Congo, another rebellion;
In Algeria, random murders on either side;
Paris a playground for thugs.

ii

The milk our children drink may or may not be poisoned
By last year's fall-out, no longer part of the news.
Our earth may be shrinking, expanding
But was found to contain great cracks
That will doubtless widen even without our help.

iii

Amid such omens
How do we dare to live?
Brashly building, begetting
For a town besieged,
Crumbling, patched again, crumbling
And undermined?

iv

Deeper I gulp cold air that not too suddenly kills,
Greedily drink with my eyes the winter sunshine and clouds,
The old white horse in the meadow
Green again after snow.

Next year I shall see no meadow, no horse.

ERRORS

A short-wave station gabbles and hums –
The newly-filled tea pot.
Turtle doves coo in the corner –
Something vibrates as I type.
Outside, a mechanical saw –
Guinea fowl screeching.
A pheasant's repeated hoot –
Cars on the new road.
I bend, and smell tom-cats –
Blackcurrant bushes;
Mimosa –
Meadowsweet.

I appoint my two eyes judge,
Sole upholders now of the decencies
Of reason, identity, place,
Yet from Thames to Riviera
Am wholly transported:
Meadowsweet to mimosa,
The blue-white-silver, yellow-tufted trees
On the mountainside
Long unvisited, never missed.
And the daily hill gone.

OLD POACHER

Learned in woods
As troubador in words,
Delicate as a troubador's lady,
Killer of does grown doe-like
In nostril, ear,
Lithely, gravely he stalks
His quarry
That will never know death.
And men stalk him.

Only a hawk cries
Above the clearing;
Robin and blackbird are still.
It is the hawk will cry
Till his eye meets
The man's eye
And silent he dips over oak-tops
In flight that is not fear
But hunger's cunning.

Fearless, wily, the man
Listens:
For dog's pad on moss, dry leaves,
Brushed fern, torn bramble,
Panting breath, cough,
Squelch of boot in trough;
Or cropped grass,
Nibble on low hazel bough,
Scuttle of hoof, claw.

And feels again
The thorny joy
Of his great indifference:
To have almost forgotten death
In the woods, in hunger's
Mastery over fear;
With senses grown
Reliable, reliant,
And a man's mind
To savour the sense –
Hunting, hunted, both hawk and deer.

AFTER ATTICA

i
Rock, rock and the sea.
Fishermen mending their nets
In the shade of tall houses
Locked up when the captains died out,
Galaxidi fell silent,
The olive trade passed it by.

At Itea now
The great barrels are filled,
The ferries loaded with strangers.
And Itea's fishermen sit
In the shade of low hovels
Mending their nets.

ii
Three vultures glide
Towards Parnassos
From the olive groves of Amphissa;
Over temple, theatre, stadium,
And the pine groves above.

The flycatcher flits
From fallen pediment
To mended pillar.
A long brown snake
Darts from loose rubble
To rooted thyme.
The holy site is a garden
For goldfinch, marigold, orchis.

Three vultures glide down
Over the valley
Where hooded crows
Perch on judas trees
To snatch the larger share.
Broken cry
Of a donkey laden with branches.

A shepherd stands in the glare,
Whistles to bell-wether, ewe,
And the lambs will follow.

Soon melted snow
Will replenish the little river
That now is an ochre track;
The swelling asphodel bulb
Will be celebrated
And, after fasting, the slaughtered lamb.
There will be dancing
To Giorgos the barber's guitar,
Neither child nor mule will be beaten
Till the women resume
Their digging, pruning, picking
That the ritual may be fulfilled.

The god who came from the sun
Has returned to the sun.
The prophetess is a cave.
The Castalian spring
Waters almond and fig tree.

The words to the song have changed.
This terrace carved out of rock
Bore a shrine, a villa, a pillbox:
Anemones bend in the breeze.
And three yellow vultures ride it
Back to the sea.

iii
In halflight
Heavy with incense
Eyes blink
At unblinking eyes,
Black symmetry
Against a heaven of gold.
King's gown and shepherd's kirtle,
Green, red and blue
Pay homage to black.
Amplified in the domed silence
The humming of bees.

Scarred by earthquake, war,
Patched and impoverished
The forecourt collects
Larger quietness
Of mountains and valley.
Heavier than incense
The fragrance of blossoming laurel.
From a shallow basin's rim
Bees drink the cold spring water.
A monk on the balcony
Reads yesterday's paper.

DEMONSTRATION IN ATHENS—
Truncheon, tear gas turned
On women, old men.
Survivors perhaps,
Defenders once of these vineyards
When three hundred were rounded up,
Herded into the shambles
To pay for one soldier's death.

And now the tourists:
A café here, a shop,
Rugs from Aráchova,
Mementoes of places missed out
Or blankly visited,
Works of art – too many –
Conceived in the camera's womb,
Undeveloped, unborn.
Their guidebooks that leap
From Oedipus at the crossroads
To our holy Luke,
Neither mention nor name those others.

So we moved our ikons
To a homely chapel,
Left to them the basilica,
Open now, and empty
Till the next coach pulls up
With click of shutters, buzz

Not of bees, but voices
Complaining of roads and hotels.

Pray for them,
Pray for eyes that blink
At unblinking eyes,
Outgazed, like us all.
That ceiling too will go
Despite our propping, patching:
May there be eyes here to blink
At the sun
And be outgazed,
Hands to water lettuce,
To tend the bees.

S-BAHN

Berlin, 1965

The gunpowder smell,
The corpses have been disposed of,
The gas rose up, diffused,
Kaiser, President, Führer
Have come and gone,
The housewives in funny hats
Came from the suburbs to shop,
Came from the central flats
To litter the woods and lakes,
Gushing about 'Natur'.
What remains is the carriage smell,
Tobacco smoke and heaters in stale air,
Indefinable, changeless
Monkey-house odour
Heavy on seats as hard
But emptier,

Now that the train connects
One desolation with another,
Punctual as ever, moves through the rubble
Of Kaiser, President, Führer,
Is halted, searched and cleared
Of those it would serve too well
This winter when, signalled on, it crosses
The frontier, no man's land,
Carrying only the smell
Over to neon lights
Past the deeper snow
Around dead financiers' villas
And the pine-woods' darkness
Into the terminus
Where one foreigner stamps cold feet.

HOMO SUM: HUMANI NIHIL ETC.

For H.M.E.

Too true. Don't say it. Don't.
Trujillo. Hero and owner of a nation,
Honoured and served by men, himself a man,
Upheld, abetted by the lords of commerce,
Dealers in sugar, dealers in carrion –
All men. What else? And the carrion also human.

To be grass, to be cud for cows. Not to know
The taste of meat or the taste of sugar,
To rise again from mud and be green,
Eat mud, eat carrion, but not with a human mouth.

NEW GODDESS

i
Mirrors line her shrines,
Full-length, for thighs, knees
To her are dedicated.

Men? They have not been abolished.
Mirrors too their eyes
Can serve the cult

When goddess, priestess in one
She treads profane ground,
Office, pavement, shop floor,

ii
Once their domain
Who now are a curious adjunct,
Useful if tame,

As poor cows to farmers once.
Oh, their god's daily tribute
Of grumbles about the cost

Of labourers, winter fodder
And vets! All those male contraptions,
Usable still

Now that farms run themselves
And what with A.I.
One bull goes a long way,

iii
Though bulls will slaver, lowing,
Farmers wheedle: love.
How the goddess laughs

Back within her walls
Of pure glass,
Water whose coolness drowned

The boy Narcissus.
Love ? The goddess alone
Is a surface-bather,

Surf-riding, wrapped
In her skin of latest cut,
Can dive skin-deep,

iv
Keep dry and consort
With mollusc, weed, fish,
Immortal until

Time, their god's invention,
Doled out by farmers once,
Oh, as love too,

Makes heavy with emptiness
Her womb, her breasts,
And the shallows, rippled,

Drag her down, down.

ORPHEUS STREET, S.E.5

i
Will they move, will they dance,
These houses put up by the money-makers
For the meek, their no-men, to breed in,
Breed money dispersed now, decayed?
And pawn shop, government surplus,
The cut price petrol station,
Dirty brick, waste paper,
Will his music gather them up?

ii
Orpheus transfigures, Orpheus transmutes all things.
His music melts walls. His music wrings
A smile from the lips of killer and nearly killed.
He wills pavements to crack. He whistles at trains,
They whimper, gasp and give up. Wherever 'it' sings
It is Orpheus – with it, well paid for his pains.
Grow, says Orpheus, and dog collars burst,
Tall factories shiver, the whole town swings.

iii
Oh, but the traffic diversions.
The road marked World's End, The West,
Runs north and east and south,
And the policeman on duty sneers:
Never mind the direction. You'll get there.
Be courteous. Be patient. If you park
Your car will be towed away.
If you walk, louts will kick in your ribs.

iv
Orpheus is peaceable. Orpheus is faithful
To the woman who was his wife,
Till she suffered a blackout, going
Down, down, where he couldn't reach her,
Where no one belongs to himself,
Far less to another. He lost her;
But loves her still, and loves everyone,
Richly paid for loving.

v

They shriek, they sob for Orpheus,
For a shred of his shirt or flesh.
He turns right, then left,
Proceeds, does a U-turn,
Turns left, turns right, turns left,
The shriek in his ears, everywhere,
He swallows a capsule, prepares
A love song, a peace song, a freedom song.

vi

The smile on her face, her smile
When he questioned her eyes for the last time
And she walked away from the stranger.
In halflight he sees no warehouse
But chasms, a river, rock.
A last glint on her hair
And the cave's darkness takes her,
Silent. Silent he leaves.

vii

Let lamp posts be trees for once,
Bend their trunks, the park benches
Fling out their limbs, let them fly,
Narrowly missing the sparrows.
Street and mind will not meet
Till street and mind go down
And the footfall that faded, faded,
Draws closer again in the dark,

viii

Lamplit or moonlit, his deathland:
Chasms, a river, rock.
The cries of children in alleyways,
The cries of birds in the air,
And the talons, innocent, tearing.
A head will float in foul water
And sing for the rubble, for her,
For the stars, for empty space.

LOACH

Loam, slimy loam, embodied, shaped,
Articulate in him. The strength, the softness.
His delicate eye draws light to riverbeds,
Through water draws our weather.

In gravel, mud, he lurks,
Gravel-coloured for safety,
Streamlined only to shoot
Back into mud or merge
In gravel, motionless, lurking.

Low he forages, late,
His radar whiskers alive
To a burrowing worm's commotion,
Tomorrow's thunder;
Advances bounding, prods
And worries a quiet pasture,
Munches athwart, in a cloud.

More than loam, at times he must rise,
His need, his weakness, richly to breathe;
Will rest on weeds, inconspicuous,
But, worse, gulp air, blow bubbles, aft,
Expose a belly naked and pale, transparent.
Stickleback, minnow
Gape at his wriggling, uncertain
Whether to nibble or flee.

Perch can swallow him whole.

OXFORD

Years on the Gothic rack:
Bells crashing down on green water,
Lashing the tree trunks for growing
The meadows for lying flat.

And the flushed girls laughing
At calf love.
Planting banderillas
That itched and dropped, but to burn –
All moved on, moved on

Not where the arches would fling them,
Not to a cloistered garden
Nor yet to the riverside,
The willows, the weeping willows,

To pins and needles in armchairs,
Shrilling of telephone, doorbell,
A well-mannered print or two
Of towers, Gothic, black
Against trim foliage, blue sky.

THE WITNESS

i

Over the telephone
From a call-box, ice-floe, raft
Comes a voice:
My name is Roberts. Yes, in a way you know me,
At least, we have met. Remember the Shetlands?
Perdita Roberts? Well, she's my mother.
They're abroad. May I call?
Good, I'll be with you in half an hour.

ii

The voice a man's.
The forgotten name a child's
With eyes coal-black as the woman's
Who put him down to play Brahms,
The Rhapsody,
In a cottage that smelled of wet wool.
Walked on the moors with her later
Towards the flickering lights,
Heard the sea roll, the sea boom
Beyond the barbed wire,
In winds one lay back on
Or charged head down;
Resisting the winds, the sea,
For time's sake, human time's,
Though out of time we walked
Away from cottage and camp, from the child asleep.
Had almost gone down in that sea
Avoiding submarines,
Kit afloat below deck,
Even the crew sick.
Before long was posted south,
Leaned on the railing, looked,
The sea calm for once.
Was she there on the quay,
The child in her arms?

iii

Twenty years old, as I was then,
He comes into my time

With no claim on my time, a stranger,
To talk of his time and mine, recall
A house in London, a bus-stop,
The taut threads linked once again, to snap –
Till now, the stranger come back,
Strangely akin, as though
The nearly drowning had been
A death as good as another,
An island, neither's home,
Had been a meeting-place
Where ice from ice had drawn
Fire, and the flickering lights
Like sunbeams had seared the moors,
His time and mine, this room
Were no more than walls raised up
Against the winds and the sea,
The sea, the winds a whisper
Loud in his ears and mine,
And we, on separate ships,
One leaving, one returning,
In neither's time going down.

FRIENDS

i

Here he sits, on the red couch
As twenty years ago on the green or blue
In a different house.
And if I shouted for joy,
Look, we are here, alive,
Wrily, faintly he'd smile:
Not to have died young
Before the dream passed through
Leaving you busy,
You with children about you,
Leaving me
Wherever I may be sitting,
Walking, standing or lying,
Eating, smoking, answering yes or no
Out of the fog into fog,
Unable to try to remember
What it was like to care
Whether and what I remembered,
Whether and what I tried –
Not to have died young
Means that the couch is red.

ii

And I think of another
Who died, with children about him,
Busy always, with words
Neither song nor speech –
Such words
As the dead might use,
Had they breath to waste –
Breathed for the dead.
Between his river, his heron
And the nearest cottage, burnt out,
The hiatus, deathly distance
Bridged by his breathing.

A harpsichord
I remember, never heard him play,
A tiled stove, he stoked it;

Old books, new pictures,
A good face, blurring.
A bundle of letters
I keep, the writing clear
While his hand rots;
And I hear his voice
Clearly, more clearly than
Ever I heard it there
In his room, looking
At the stove, the pictures,
His harpsichord.

iii
Our loyalty, old friend, is to the dark
As yet again we walk the same few streets
Past the same grimy hedges,
New cars, new dogs and glossier paint on doors,
Hardly to notice them, or how this wall has crumbled,
But talk as ever of taxes and conscription,
Small victories, small defeats.
And though for twenty-five years you have been saying,
What will become of us,
Too well you know it, meaning not us at all
But his regalia, or else the many things,
Real things, regalia of the working day
We care about, only because we know
How poor the realm is, how mad our king.

He dreams, and abdicates,
Leaving no heir, the currency in doubt,
Crying: The King is dead. Long live dead kings –
Lords, by divine right, over dodo and mammoth,
Rulers of nettles, commanders of lava,
Defenders of icebergs adrift in forgotten gales.

Poor capital. Poor streets that still we walk.
Mad king who laughs at those who serve him
And, re-instated, longs for a larger kingdom.
We're nothing in his dream. His dream is ours.

AT FIFTY-FIVE

Country dances
Bird calls
The breathing of leaves after thunder –
And now fugues.
Modulations 'impolite'
Syncopations 'unnatural'.
No more clapping of hands
When moonshine had opened their tear-ducts
Or fanfares clenched
Heroic nerves –
But a shaking of heads:
Can't help it, our decomposer,
Can't hear his own blundering discords.

As if one needed ears
For anything but chitchat about the weather,
Exchange of solicitude, malice –
And birdsong, true, the grosser, the bouncing rhythms.
Uncommunicative? Yes. Unable
'Like beginners to learn from nightingales'.
Unwilling, too, for that matter –
To perform, to rehearse, to repeat,
To take in, to give back.

In time out of time, in the concert no longer concerted.
But the music all there, what music,
Where from –
Water that wells from gravel washed clean by water.
All there – inaudible thrushes
Outsinging the nightingales, peasants
Dancing weightless, without their shoes –
Where from, by what virtue? None.
By what grace but still being here, growing older?
The water cleansed by gravel washed clean by water.

Fugue, ever itself –
And ever growing,
Gathering up – itself,
Plunging – into itself,
Rising – out of itself,

Fathoming – only itself
To end, not to end its flowing –
No longer itself –
In a stillness that never was.

DOWLAND

Pleasant are the tears which music weeps
And durable, black crystal, each drop keeps
When eyes are dry a glimmer of deep light,
But melting, mixed with wine,
Could move the great to offer gold for brine.
Miraculous exchange!
Until that trade grew strange,
Mere dearth of common bread,
True tears, true absence drained the fountainhead,
Put out in utter night,
The glimmer, lost to their eyes, lost to mine.
And then I knew what trade
I'd practised unbeknown:
Of blood not ink was my black music made,
Feigned grief to them so sweet because my own
Transmuted nolens volens
By cruel mastery's menial, semper dolens.
But tearless I depart,
Glad that my lute melts no time-serving heart
And deep in crystal glows dark Dowland's art.

FOR A FAMILY ALBUM

Four heads in one lamp's light
And each head bowed into peculiar darkness,
Reading, drawing, alone.
A camera would have caught them, held them there
Half-lit in the room's warm halflight,
Left them, refused to tell
How long till that lamp was broken,
Your hair pinned up or cut or tinted or waved.

I cannot even describe them, caught no more
Than a flash of light that ripped open
The walls of our half-lit room;
Or the negative – a black wedge
Rammed into light so white that it hurt to look.

Leave this page blank.
You'd neither like nor believe
The picture no lens could have taken:

Tied to my rooted bones
In your chairs you were flying, flying.

GREY HEAT

Grey heat, but a breeze blends
Day lily with evening primrose,
Bronzed orange with purest lemon.

Care lasts longer, and longer
The town's blend of grey,
The rise, the crumbling of brickwork.

Less long the thrust of a spade at the roots,
The blows of great hammers on housefronts,
The grey sea wave that licks the light from your eyes.

Dare look, presume to believe
The blending of day-long petals,
Momentous whim of a breeze.

THE HOUSE MARTINS

Pines I remember, the air crisp.
Here, in a haze, elms I see,
Do not see, and hills hiding the river.

But the roof is generous,
Can preserve nests. And again the martins mutter
Their small-talk, daily domestic twitter
After those miles, deadly to some,
Over glaciers, over high waves.

Arrived, arrived in whatever wind,
To ride all winds and, housed on the windy side,
Warm with their own blood the old mud walls.

THE JACKDAWS

Gone, I thought, had not heard them for years;
Gone like the nuthatch, the flycatcher,
Like the partridges from the bulldozed hill.
Now it was I who was going,
And they were back, or had never gone,
Chucking, bickering up on the elm's bare branches.

I forgot the changes, the chores,
Jackdaw's corpse in the water tank,
Jackdaw's nest, jackdaw's dry bones, dry feathers
Stuffed down the chimneys –
No longer mine to clear.
I heard them, I saw them again in the cold clean air
And, going, my tenure ended,
Brought in the harvest of three thousand weathers,
The soot, the silver, their hubbub on trees left behind.

Red house on the hill.
Windward, the martins' mud nests
Year after year filled
With a twittering, muttering brood.
On the still side, hedged,
Appled turned in on themselves
A damp, dull summer long
Until ripe. Rare hum of bees.
The two great elms where the jackdaws roosted,
Beyond them the wild half-acre
With elm scrub rising, rambling
From old roots –
Never tamed or possessed
Though I sawed, scythed, dug
And planted sapling, walnut,
Hazel, sweet chestnut,
A posthumous grove.
And the meadow's high grass,
Flutter of day-moth over
Mallow, cranesbill, vetch:
All razed, bole and brick,
Live bough and empty nest,
Battered, wrenched, scooped
Away to be dumped, scrapped.

ii
A place in the mind, one place in one or two minds
Till they move on, confused, cluttered with furniture, landmarks.
The house let me go in the end, sprung no more leaks or cracks,
The garden ceased to disown me with bindweed, ground elder.

What's left is whole: a sketch or two, a few photographs,
A name on old maps. And the weather. The light.

iii
Seeing martins fly
Over a tiled roof, not mine,
Over concrete, tarmac,

A day-moth cling
To a nettle flower,
Hearing children, not mine,
Call out in a laurel-hedged orchard,
I'm there again. Home.

VII
Consumed
1969-1972

GONE

*Thomas Good: born Beeston, Notts., Oct. 29th 1901;
missing from Richmond, Surrey, since Jan. 20th 1970*

i
'The presence of 200 guests,
Many of them only waiting
To die, depresses me.
I have not had the strength
To go to London. But
I hope to leave
After the 15th of January.
If I remember rightly,
February is like
A little springtime.
The other plans
I shall put off
Till April.'
                My luggage
Has failed me here
Against a room worn
As my clothes, my books,
Manuscripts thumbed
By indifferent men
And returned. How long, how far
I have shifted them
Across the frontiers, decades,
Only to bring them here,
Home, Terminus Hall
Where no one dances
To penny whistle or gramophone,
A decorous quiet obtains
And the wallpaper, worn,
Repeats in weary tones
Its admonition:
                Rest.
Give up your journeys,
Give up your jumbled loves,
Lady of Pimlico,
Lady of Beirut
Who in Oxford and Aix and Verona and everywhere

Smiled from a bus,
Nodded high on a horse
As you fluttered on
With your phrases picked
From an earlier dawn's adoration,
Skipped with a joy
Your churchy youth forbade,
When the coin was valid.

Well, yes, I spent my life leaping
From memories to plans,
From loss to recollection.
This room clamps me
To the empty space between . . .

ii
Once more he packed. With meticulous care
Though his mind was wandering out to the streets of wintry
    London,
Loitering on doorsteps of houses demolished by bombs,
Faltering over doorbells that no one he knew could answer,
North, by the Midlands, to Filey 'surrounded by landscapes
That enchant me more and more', south again to Sussex,
And over the Channel, rivers, mountains, Mediterranean Sea,
While his hands disposed
Diary, wallet, passport, tobacco tin filled with coins,
Things he had done with. Paid his rent to the day,
Put on his raincoat and beret, walked out,
Leaving all he possessed, and one library book, overdue.

iii
Feeling that void grow
Best filled with earth,
In old age or sickness a cat
From house to thicket will drag it,
Under a laurel hedge, close
To the roots will sit,
Nothing more in her gaze
Than a meek waiting,
Alone with it and the air's
Hummed continuum
Ever the same, from birth.

Could he, tunes in his head,
Busoni, music-hall,
Words in his head,
Heard and read,
Lie down or fall, hide
From eyes inside him
Of his living, his dead?
To what earth, what water, where
In a city not pitiless
Creep into animal time
Unowned, untenanted?

iv
'There is hardly a climate in England
That suits me; and where to settle
I have not the least idea.
I am not allowed
To draw my pension abroad'.
And yet, to keep moving,
Mind and body at one
Till mind stops, body drops
Is freedom of a kind.
I cannot help it, this joy
That gathers me up to defy
The better judgement of walls,
Gathers all I have been,
All I have loved, and drives me
I don't know where, to rest,
I don't know where, to die.

THAMES

Good river, it carries
Food for men, for gulls.

Beautiful river
This winter evening
It melts into mauves and greys
Tower, chimney, wharf,
A mirror breathed upon
By haze and the lips of lovers.

This afternoon I saw
My friend's face, purple
After forty days of drifting
Between cold banks, in the brown water;

And drove home, along
The Embankment where he
Had breathed, loitered, loved
In a haze, mauves and greys
While the refuse of gulls, of men
Slapped the black bulk of barges.

White-faced, but with fuel enough,
With food enough to keep going.
Today, tomorrow not far from the river,
Still able at times to be fooled,

Down through the rippled lamplight
I drive, into real mud.

DUST

i
Living with it, till the flakes
Are thick enough to pick up
With my fingers and drop
Into wastepaper basket, bin
Or bowl, whichever is nearest,
Must I recant, take back
My 'hymns to dusters' (unwritten)
Now that she they were meant for dusts
Another man's rooms? A traitor,
In turn, not to her but all
Those heroic housewives, charwomen,
Worldwide relentless army
Fighting the stuff with equipment
So various, intricate, fussy,
It scares me, as dust does not?
Dropped out, for good, from that unending campaign,
Their daily advance by inches,
Their nightly retreat by as many
Or more; the chemical warfare,
The cleaning of cleaning utensils,
Maintenance of the means of maintaining
What never can be maintained.

No, I'll revoke nothing,
Not even revoked love,
Things that dust blurs or dust
Blown away uncovers,
Awed, as before, by the valour
Of grappling till death with death;
But, tainted, feel free to prefer
The smell of dust to the smell
Of disinfectants, polish,
Floor-cloth and mop, breathing in
Matter's light breath, exhalation
That mingles pollen with down,
Germs with ashes, and falls
On my brooms, my vacuum cleaner,
On the whiteness of pillow, paper,

135

Unendingly falls, whirls,
Drifts or settles, fertile
And deadly, like being alive.

ii
And yet in a dream I see them,
The dreamers of reason, the cleaners
Humanly march to the coast
Of every ocean on earth
To clear the beaches, reform
Those flotsam-retching waters,
Their seaweed-killer guns
Cocked in the cause of order.

The music I hear, dreaming,
Is canon, fugue, ricercare,
No slop, no loose ends.
If they sing there, under
A cloudless sky, while they let
Pure sand run through their fingers,
The waves hold back, it is:
Veni creator spiritus,
Antibiotic, make us
More than the dust that we are.
Lest we lie too long in bed,
Day-dreaming, of night,
Of nature's way with our flesh,
Come, spirit, and destroy
What merely lives and dies;
Give us the dream of reason.

I wake to the howling of winds.
To darkness. I breathe dust.

Where are you, girl, under the whole hulk
Of smooth flesh unused, the figurehead eyes
Pale blue enamel, staring, no laughter, no tears
To rise from within against lamplight, daylight
And refract them, playing?
Your lips are composed, for death.
When they part and the life in you finds a word
It is death, it is going down into sleep
And beyond, you're that far away, and there
You look for yourself.
                       I look for you here,
Speak your name, beg you to stay, to wait,
For what, you ask, and I know
With electric currents they tore you
Out of your mad speed,
Joy of a kind, a fury, a pain,
And now with narcotics moor you
To where you are not.
                    Why don't you die, is your answer,
As if there we could meet,
Or else to be rid of me
Trying to hold you, fighting
The undertow, tug of more than your weight
Together with it.
                But where are you,
Where can I reach you with words,
With tongue or finger touch you and make you feel
So that you move again, if only to drift
With the water and winds that are passing you by?

It's your self-love you have lost,
Unloving, and I cannot serve it unloved.
Yet listen for once, tell me
What the place is like where diminished
You long to be less. Let the telling
Cut you loose for your own way.

MAD LOVER, DEAD LADY

Oh, my Diotima.
Is it not my Diotima you are speaking of?
Thirteen sons she bore me, one of them is Pope,
Sultan the next, the third is the Czar of Russia.
And do you know how it went with her?
Crazy, that's what she went, crazy, crazy, crazy.

Thirteen funerals they gave me when I died.
But she was not there. Locked up in a tower.
That's how it goes: round the bend
Out of the garden where lovers meet,
Walking, talking together. Over the wall.
No one there. Till you visitors come:
Will the corpse write a poem today
About his mad lady?

But I'll tell you a secret: we meet.
Round the bend, on the other side of the wall
Our garden is always there,
Easy, with every season's flowers.
Each from a dark street we come
And the sun shines.
She laughs when I tell her
What it's like to be dead.
I laugh when she gives me
News of our crazy children
Who've made their way in the world.

No poem today, sir.
Go home. In a dream you'll see
How they remove themselves, your dead
Into madness. And seem to forget
Their loved ones, each in his own dark street.
How your mad loved ones
Seem to forget their dead.
That's how it goes. No one there.
Oh, my Diotima.
Waiting for me in the garden.

ROSES, CHRYSANTHEMUMS

It's late in the day, in the year,
The frost holding off, just.
In the garden you pick dry stalks, hardly looking.
Time to come in,
Time to pick flowers, only now,
And carry them in, summer and autumn bunched,
Toward winter, even the full roses' petals
In no hurry to fall.

It is a slow music we hear
Behind the wind. And the chrysanthemums
Are a slow fire,
A red so dark it glimmers and would go out
But for the yellow that radiates from the core.
Ruffled flutterings here, a harsh odour
As of wood-smoke, and there
Flesh colour, silky, taut in its bland breathing,
Linger and mingle.

Now. Only now.

THE SEWING

There was no saying it, you
Found and lost in the time it takes
To open and shut a door,
How every stitch stabbed;
No uttering, crying out
The now, now, now
Without before or after
But what the now could have made.
Had I died there, then,
That would have been true;
Not to mend, as words must,
The break with a thread.

There is no telling it now,
Or ever, to you, though I must
In words that will break again
Only because I live, driving or walking
Through the streets of a different town,
A carrier for coats that need buttons.
And the now is never, never,
The corner passed daily, twice,
With a buttoned coat, to be stabbed,
Far off, the thread loose.

Here's nothing, then: true words
Turned into lies by the lacked act.

LOVE

It ought to make mystics of us,
This concentration of all that we are and have
On nothing.
But I can't talk. Though my life flowed out to you
In words, while you lay
With another, at peace, happy,
What's ink compared to the juice
Which, more promptly undeceived, I might have spilt
For nothing.

If we must fall into it, for it,
No man was luckier than the near-mystic
Who at eighty-two years
Poured his love out in pints of blood
From the heart, lungs, mouth,
And died on his mistress, in bed,
Before she could leave him
With nothing.

You I write, even now, as though
Having words left, tenderness, folly unspent,
I owed them to you still
And hadn't given enough
To nothing
When happy, at peace in your presence I couldn't know
That had my blood splotched your body, soured the half-lies on your lips
Within hours you'd have washed it off, clean and new for another –
Another way of losing yourself
In nothing.

ODE TO JOY

You're somewhere, they tell me, hiding
Only from me. When I say you've gone, moved out
They show me benches, floors,
Doorsteps, the stone of back yards
You sleep on now. Hint that I may have seen you
And walked by, no eyelash left of your features
To blink recognition and, blinking, be recognized.
Brag that they meet you, know you, have made you
Their mescalin bride, for moments deep and delicate as you were
To me when one house could hold you,
One mirror suffice you, one garden was yours
Even in winter, the last of your heelmarks
Blindly divined under snow.

Hide? How can you, so near?
The less he courted you then
The more you amazed your long-faced lover
Come from his black pudding dinner, his raventail party
Down streets where the lamps had failed, by being there,
Waiting in candlelight, faithful to him.
Could leave for a sunny country, lock up,
Write him no postcard for weeks, for a month or longer
And return with a present, unchanged.
He, for the shareholders, meanwhile had itemized that year's trading losses,
Balanced their total against the depreciation of assets
And declared a minus dividend –
Coolly lugubrious. He could count on you.

All right. We're older. The dirtier air
Blocks or thickens the waves you transmitted.
Computers will plot a course
For the homing of homeless migrants,
The wildflowers you looked for will blossom on paper.
But call on me once, as different as you like,
As briefly, casually. Caring so little now
Where you are, with whom, you will hardly notice
What strangers we have become. We need not talk
If I hear you breathe in this room, this world,
Light finds a shape to outline,
A body to shine on, to shade.

CONSUMED

The fault was impatience to live, burning,
The fault was joy that flashes and strikes, burning

And made this hollow where now the creature
Hibernates in my heart and guts.
Not that I let it in – I have never seen it.
If it was there from the start
It must have been free to slip out and return,
Feed and breed, run across turf, moss,
Leap or drop from one tree on to another.

Curled up now it sleeps; will twitch, as though dreaming
But not budge. Sustained by its own fat
Retches when I eat, turns every food against me.
What protrudes is my bones. No bulge betrays
How the creature thrives inside me.
Yet women, warned by a handshake, look,
Sense the redundant presence, and keep away.

When spring comes the creature will stir, leave me,
The hollow hurt again, ache to be filled.
Joy will strike again, burning,
And finish me off.

THE GLADE

i

All day in the glare, on the salt lake's beaches,
All night in a fever, shaking.
That's done with. My travels are over.
Somehow I'm here: glade in a dense wood.
Leafage makes lace. The shadows are of it, in it,
The season is everymonth.
White sorrel around me, and white anemone,
Foxglove purple, strawberry red.
Apple shapes, pear shapes have lasted all winter.
And the snow gleams above dry moss.

You don't see it, you cannot see it,
Travelling still to a town the guidebook foretells:
How it is to have gone and returned and gone
And returned and forgotten to go
And forgotten the route and the place
And be there again, and be everywhere.

Stay with me, love, till my fingers have traced the landscape
On your body and into your mind.

ii

May we lie there, you ask; and how long.
By the hour, for ever, on a bed leased
From the turning trees and the conifers.
Leaving again and again,
Again and again left
To the dark and the whorled light.

Can you bear the silence between us?
You're of it, love, you are in it.
When I touch you I touch the silence,
When I've lost you it turns to me.

So late, nothing can part us:
We belong to the glade.

VIII
Travelling
1967-1972

TRAVELLING I

i
Mountains, lakes. I have been here before
And on other mountains, wooded
Or rocky, smelling of thyme.
Lakes from whose beds they pulled
The giant catfish, for food,
Larger, deeper lakes that washed up
Dead carp and mussel shells, pearly or pink.
Forests where, after rain,
Salamanders lay, lopped the dark moss with gold.
High up, in a glade,
Bells clanged, the cowherd boy
Was carving a pipe.

And I moved on, to learn
One of the million histories,
One weather, one dialect
Of herbs, one habitat
After migration, displacement,
With greedy lore to pounce
On a place and possess it,
With the mind's weapons, words,
While between land and water
Yellow vultures, mewing,
Looped empty air
Once filled with the hundred names
Of the nameless, or swooped
To the rocks, for carrion.

ii
Enough now, of grabbing, holding,
The wars fought for peace,
Great loads of equipment lugged
To the borders of bogland, dumped,
So that empty-handed, empty-minded,
A few stragglers could stagger home.

And my baggage – those tags, the stickers
That brag of a Grand Hotel
Requisitioned for troops, then demolished,

Of a tropical island converted
Into a golf course;
The specimens, photographs, notes –
The heavier it grew, the less it was needed,
The longer it strayed, misdirected,
The less it was missed.

iii
Mountains. A lake.
One of a famous number.
I see these birds, they dip over wavelets,
Looping, martins or swallows,
Their flight is enough.
The lake is rough,
To be here, forgetful,
In a boat, on water,
The famous dead have been here.
They saw and named what I see,
They went and forgot.

I climb a mountainside, soggy,
Then springy with heather.
The clouds are low,
The shaggy sheep have a name,
Old, less old than the breed
Less old than the rock
And I smell hot thyme
That grows in another country,
Through gaps in the Roman wall
A cold wind carries it here,

iv
Through gaps in the mind,
Its fortifications, names:
Name that a Roman gave
To a camp on the moor
Where a sheep's jawbone lies
And buzzards, mewing, loop
Air between woods and water
Long empty of his gods;
Name of the yellow poppy
Drooping, after rain,

Or the flash, golden,
From wings in flight –
Greenfinch or yellowhammer –

Of this mountain, this lake. I move on.

TRAVELLING II

i
A hybrid region. I walk half-seeing,
Half-hearing the mourning dove,
The mocking-bird's range of innate
And of mimed music, jumbled.
Here the dogwood grows wild, and here
It was planted, flowering pink
Above gaudy azaleas, in gardens
Carved out of hillside and forest.

Red clay. White sand. Meagre pines.
If no copperhead basked
On trails a Cherokee cut, no tortoise
Lurched over fallen branches
I might be back where I started.
Three thousand miles back. And colder.

ii

Thirty years back. Three hundred.
It's the same earth,
With beer can openers lying
Inches away from arrowheads,
Flint, and fossils barely covered.
The sameness confuses. If now
A rabbit screamed I'd be elsewhere,
By Thames or Windrush or Taw,
Moving as now I move
Through one death to the next.

On the one bank of the Bea,
Oak, beech, thickly bunched,
I half-see, on the other
Spruce, larch, for pit props,
Their thin trunks planted, with gaps
For a black light.
Over both buzzards loop.

iii

By the Yare I called
On my father thirty years dead
In a city. From his bombed house
He'd retired, into a shack
With holes in the roof, gaps
In the board walls. Alone,
He was rapt, absorbed
In his new profession of nothingness,
And needed no calls, no concern;
Had forgotten so much,
I could not speak, looked on,
Looked around and left, quietly.

Still those words rot in my mouth
Which I did not speak, and others,
Unspoken, spoken, of caring,
For ever mocked as I stepped
Out of indifference fulfilled
Into a street, path, track
From which time peeled away
And yesterday's name had been swept
Together with yesterday's paper.

iv

And yet I speak to you, love,
Write words for you. Can you read them?
Can you bear them, bear with me there
Or here, anywhere?
Can you keep them from falling, hold them
In a place become yours, real?

It's the same earth we walk,
Variously lost,
You from the dogwood, white-flowering,
I from the thin pines,
With many rivers between us,
Ocean between us, one.
To meet you I move on,
Sorting, throwing out words
Only so that the one
May prove sound, yours,

v

One place contain us, a whole year,
Our spring and fall, our growth and our dying
Be like your breath when you stand
Arrested, your eyes
Darkening, widening to reflect
And draw in, drown what's around them;

Wholly to see, hear again
And be here, there, wholly.
For that alone I walk
The named and nameless roads
Through tame and wild woods,
Along the banks of so many rivers
Too much the same till we meet.

TRAVELLING III

i

No, it's over, our summer,
Part of a summer, you gone
Across the Channel with too much luggage,
Making your way back
To dogwood, red-berried now,
To nights warm still and loud
With whippoorwill, crickets,
And I about to go
Where maples begin to turn,
In half-sleep katydid, katydid
Grates out a brainless reminder
Of what and what, meet you, will not.

The sun has come out again
Here, in the same garden
That's turning too, never the same
One whole day, one whole hour.
Gales have snapped off
The last early pear
And, darkening, the goldenrod withers.
Over there it's budding, wild,
Like phlox, long withered here,
But without you where am I?
Neither here nor there, and the names
Dissolve, garden and meadow float
Out of my reach together,
Different, the same, both remote.

ii

You move on, looking,
Finding something to feel
Here or there, anywhere,
Collect and lose, recollect
And like the more for the losing
That makes it more your own.
How you rush through Rome
In a morning, to see, to see,
To have seen, to have been
Where the names tell you you were,

Then, moving still, gather
What the names will not hold.

You got it home, your too heavy luggage,
Unpacked, and put away
Our summer, part of a summer,
Left again and for lodging chose
A trailer. You hinted:
An alias now was the name
That loving had learnt you by.

iii
My travels, true, are unlearning,
An unloading of this piece and that,
Shedding of names, needs.
But the last have the pull of earth,
Of the earth we walk, our foothold.
Break them, and we fly or go under.

Almost the lightness came,
Almost the bareness in which
'The worst returns to laughter'.
I wait. The days drag,
Heavy, and long, long.
The laughter I hear is not mine,
My lightness no more than the weight
It was driven away from, a drifting
Between indifferent shores
Through this autumn now hot, now cold,
With the sky clouding over, clearing,
As if there could be no end,
Only the turning, clinging of leaves to stalk,
Of flesh to bone,

iv
Though for hunger I needed your tongue,
For wanting to touch, your fingers,
For wanting, wanting you,
For looking, your hungry eyes,
For rest, their drowsing, their closing,
For bare words, your listening,
For destination, you,

Not here, not there, not anywhere
To be reached now,
So fast you rush on, away from
The place that, holding you still,
Could fill and affirm your name,

v

As I pack again, off at last,
For a while yet to travel,
Go and return, unlearning.
At their lightest the leaves fall,
At their lightest glide on the wind.

But enough now. More than enough
Of pressing into words
What sense, cluttered or stripped,
And mind leave behind them:
Mountains, lakes, rivers,
Too many, and you,
One, but moved on,
Nameless to me because named
You'd evade the name.

Here, in the same garden,
Branches are barer,
The late pears ripe.
No frost yet. Heavy
The grass droops, damp.
I wait, learning to stay.

TRAVELLING IV

i
In winter light, walled
With glass too thin to hold
Any motion but memory's
That displaces no bulk, breaks
No surface, fills
No space, leaves no trace,
Litter or wake,

Travelling, stay
As Earth does, fixed,
And staying travel
As Earth does, revolving.

ii
Earth. That must be the name
Still. Light. Air.
Walking the city I noted
That men live on light, air
Still, even here, unless
Filtering eyes or lungs
Fail, and waste clogs them,
Killing. The sun gets through
Still, the luckier poor can sit
On doorsteps, look up and see
A strip of sky they could almost
Feel to be common property.
A wind in those parts can cross
The river, cold, but bringing
Air nearly as good as new.
As nearly pure as the water
Rich people buy, canned.

iii
Where am I? Bare trees
On a slope. Between the trunks,
Forked or single, islands of green,
Moss-green brighter than snow
Against leaf-brown, and evergreen,
Glossily dark, of laurel and

Rhododendron. Between shrieks,
A bluejay's, one call recurs,
High, low, low, low, the fall
Chromatic, moan of the
Mourning dove.

America,
East, with a little voice
Unfolding an emptiness, huge,
Though trucks roar through it, sirens,
Foghorns defy, define it.

iv
And you? How near
In space, and more deaf
To me than my dead are.
So that now if I speak
It is of the emptiness, in a voice
Damped as the dove's in winter,
Of the emptiness only. But there,
If anywhere, you are listening,

Part of it, never more
Than half-born into place,
Time, from a region
Watery, leafy, dreamed
Before the cities were built.

v
Too late I take back
Those words and names
Of place, time, spoken
To bind you, to bend you
Awake. A mending, you said,
And left and hid from me. Where?
Awake? Or lost now,
The next quarter of birth
Too sudden, a wrenching, a rending
Away from the shapes of conch,
Pebble, tendril and frond
That molded your mind?

Not to know, your need now,
To creep into what remains
Of sleep, not to be known?

Enough of grabbing, holding,
Of our fidgety greed.
Clutter that men dump
On to Earth, into Earth
Until no cure will work
But beyond herself
To unload, explode her.

vi
Last of my needs, you
I'll unlearn, relinquish
If that was love. Too late,
Let you go, return, stay
And move on. Let you be,
Nameless.

Begin again, saying:
Mountain, Lake. Light.
Earth. Water. Air.
You. Nothing more. No one's.

TRAVELLING V

i
Now or before, when the dogwood flowered
And you came walking out of no street or house
Known to me, with a gift
So much more than itself that the promise
Could not be kept. But the loan
Was mine, to consume like the air
Of that 'sweete and most healthfullest climate',
Yours while you walk there, changed,
Breathing its loan of air,
And the dogwood flowers
Where other trees grew,
'Great, tall, soft, light
And yet tough enough I think to be fitte
Also for masts of shippes'
Of the kind sunk by sandbanks,
Battered by hurricanes there,
At the wild cape.

Gone, lost, the trees and the ships,
The possession and hope of possession;
Found, through the giving up,
Where I'm not, on the white sands,
A shell in her hand, she, 'for ever fair'.

ii
I move on, closer now to the end
That is no end as long as
One mountain remains, one lake,
One river, one forest
Yet to be named, possessed,
Relinquished, forgotten, left
For Earth to renew. Move on
To no end but of 'I', 'you'
And the linking words, love's,
Though love has no end,
Though words, when the link is broken,
Move on beyond 'I' and 'you',

iii
As do his, who forsook the place,
His traffic island where love
Set up house and raised orphans,
Tenderly taught them to till
The hardest rock. Yet, after so much,
Gave in, to his blood's revolt
Against veins, against the heart
Pushing its dope, pumping
And pumping hope
Out into limbs that had learnt,
From things touched, to be still.
Could not eat now, the new bread
That tasted of flesh left unburied
Decades, frontiers ago,
Could not drink now, the new wine
That tasted of salt,
From a dry sea,
From a blinded eye,

And, slowly, began to go
Where he must, where
His poems had gone before him,
Into silence now, silence,
Water at last, water
Which, unclean, could wash
All it flows over, fills,
Even his mouth, of the last words,
And move on.

iv
Slowly, detained by love,
He went, but never
Slowly enough for Earth
In her long slow dream
That has not finished yet
With the gestation of man,
The breaker of her dream,
And has not finished
Digesting the teeth and bones
Of her dinosaurs.

Making and breaking words,
For slowness,
He opened gaps, for a pulse
Less awake, less impatient
Than his, who longed
To be dreamed again,
Out of pulverized rock,
Out of humus,
Bones, anthropoid, saurian,
And the plumage of orioles;
Cleared a space, for the poems
That Earth might compose
'On the other side
Of mankind'
And our quick ears
Could not hear.

v

Gone. Lost. Half-forgotten already
What quick eyes took in,
Quick hands felt the shape of, tongue
Touched with a name. Half-forgotten
The oriole's drab call
High up, on the crest of a flowering pear-tree,
A month or two back, not here,
Not in the city garden
Where from a drabber throat
A thrush luxuriantly warbles and foxgloves
Find a wood, though the woods were felled.